MAGADHAN LITERATURE

Owing to the antiquity and rarity of this book, certain pages are regrettably absent, and readability is compromised due to the blurring of the original text. If you possess any insights regarding the availability of these missing sections, kindly inform us. Your assistance is crucial in ensuring the completion of this significant work for the benefit of future generations.

MAGADHAN LITERATURE

BEING

A COURSE OF SIX LECTURES
DELIVERED AT PATNA UNIVERSITY
IN
DECEMBER 1920 AND APRIL 1921

BY

MAHAMAHOPADHYAY

HARA PRASAD SASTRI,

M.A., C.I.E.

GYAN

Published by

Gyan Publishing House
5, Ansari Road
Daryaganj, New Delhi-110002
Phone: 011-47034999, 9811692060
E-mail: books@gyanbooks.com

Distribution Network
gyanbooks.com
India, USA, Canada, UK, Australia

ISBN: 978-93-6280-273-6 (PB)
First Published, 1923

2nd Impression 2024

Printed at: Gyan Press, Delhi.

MAGADHAN LITERATURE
Author: HARA PRASAD SASTRI

MAGADHAN LITERATURE

BEING

A COURSE OF SIX LECTURES

DELIVERED AT PATNA UNIVERSITY

IN

DECEMBER 1920 AND APRIL 1921

BY

MAHAMAHOPADHYAY HARAPRASAD SASTRĪ, M.A., C.I.E.,
Professor of Sanskrit, Dacca University.

CALCUTTA:

PRINTED AT THE HARE PRESS AND PUBLISHED
BY THE PATNA UNIVERSITY, PATNA.

1923

TABLE OF CONTENTS

MAGADHAN LITERATURE.

Lecture I.

Original Inhabitants of Magadha.

The vast territory to the South of the Ganges and North of the Vindhya ranges extending from Mudgagiri (Monghyr) in the East to the Charaṇādri (Chunar) in the West is called Magadha. The tract lying between Karmanāśa and Chunar, however, is often joined to Kāśí on the opposite side of the river.

The word Kíkaṭa occurs once only in the Ṛg-Veda. III. 53. 14. and as the word Kíkaṭa in later literature meant Magadha or a part of it from Chunār to Rājgir (Visva Koṣa, from Sakti Sangama-Tantra). Many are disposed to think that the word Kíkaṭa in Ṛg-Veda means Magadha. The references to Kíkaṭa in later literature are the following:—

कीकटो नाम देशोऽनार्य्यनिवासः। निरुक्त[1]
बुद्धो नाम्ना जिनसुतः कीकटेषु भविष्यति।[2]
कीकटेषु गया पुण्या नदी पुण्या पुनः पुना।
च्यवनस्याश्रमः पुण्यः पुण्यं राजगृहं वनं॥

These certainly refer to Magadha, but the scene of the hymn in the Ṛg-Veda in which the word occurs, is laid in the vicinity of the Indus (Sindhu). It is a far cry from Indus to Magadha. In the whole of the Ṛg-Veda, the easternmost points mentioned are, Gangā and Yamunā

---

[1] Satyavrata Vol. III. p. 273.

[2] Bhagavat I. 3. 24.

(Jumna), most probably their southern courses from the mountains. The word Kíkaṭa is explained once as a proper name by Sāyaṇa—

अनार्य्यनिवासेषु जनपदेषु

and a second time as *Nāstikas* (Atheists), who have no faith in religious ceremonies. The only thing which the Ṛg-Veda mentions about the Kíkaṭas is their kine, which, the hymnist regretfully mentions, are of no use in Soma sacrifice. Yet he covets them to use their milk for sacrificial purposes. It is a well-known fact that the best kine in India are to be found within a few scores of miles from the Indus in the districts of Hissar, Sirsa, Bhawalpore and Bikaner and it is most probable that these places are mentioned as Kíkaṭa and not Magadha. The theory that Pramaganda was the founder of the kingdom of Magadha and that the word Magadha is another form of "Maganda" in Pramaganda occuring in the same ṛk, is to say the least of it, ridiculous.

The country is called Magadha in the Kauṣítakí Áraṇyaka[1] and that the Kauṣítakís had a close connection with this country will be explained later. The Atharva-Veda has Magadhas, the plural denoting a tribe.[2] This tribe was not very friendly to the Vedic Aryans as the Atharva-Veda thinks that Malarial Fever should be driven away to Magadhas as beyond the pale of Vedic civilization. One Śākhā of the Veda joins the Aṅgas with the Magadhas and the other Śākhā joins the Kāśis with them. It is from this tribe, that in the Kauṣítakí Áraṇyaka we get the name of the country as Magadha. Some think that Bagadha mentioned with Baṅga and Chera in the Aitareya Áraṇyaka[3] is only another form of Magadha.

---

[1] VII. 13. [2] V. 22. 14. [3] II. 1. 1.

But this does not seem to be tenable. For, between Banga and Chera or the Dravidian people in Chutia-Nagpur, the whole country—now Burdwan Division—has in it a powerful ethnical race still called Bāgdís, which is another form of Bagadha. They form altogether an ethnos with peculiar features and peculiar colour. They are tall, stout, robust and war-like. They had a government of their own and I have reason to think that they had a language of their own, too. So, from the tribe Magadhas, the country received the name Magadha. The word Māgadha means an inhabitant of Magadha, not necessarily belonging to the tribe of Magadhas. The Māgadhas are neither Brahmanas nor Śūdras (Vāja. Saṁ. 30.22), and they are to be sacrificed in the Puruṣamedha to the god Atikruṣṭa ("Loud Noise.")[1] The humour of the thing lies in the fact that the Māgadhas made loud noise in their songs. The word Māgadha later meant minstrels, who lived by singing loudly the praise of kings ; and the Bhāṭs of Rājputānā and other provinces who claimed their descent from the Māgadhas make a huge noise when they sing the praises of the donors of gifts. The noise is often intolerable.

In the Vrātya chapter of the Atharva-Veda[2] the Māgadha is said to be a friend and adviser, a crony and a thunder of the Vrātya (*mitra*, *mantra*, *hasa* and *stanayitnu*) and this is the character which the Bhāṭas and Chāraṇas are still maintaining in Rājputāna. When the Vrātyas and Māgadhas are so intimately connected and when Vrātyas are enjoined to give away all their property to *Magadhadeśiya Brahmabandhu* in some of the Sūtras, it becomes necessary to see who the Vrātyas were. The

---

[1] Vāj Saṃ XXX. 5. 22.

[2] XV.

word is often explained as *Sāvitrí-patitāḥ*[1]—those who do not utter Gāyatrī. Those who explain the word in this way seem to have in the back of their mind, the notion that the word is derived from *vrata*. But it cannot be derived from the word *vrata*. There is no rule by which a negative can be asserted by a Taddhita suffix. So, I think, it should be derived from the word *Vrāta*, a horde.

The word Vrāta is eight times used in the Ṛg-Veda, thrice in the family maṇḍalas—the oldest portions of the Ṛg-Veda,—thrice in the tenth maṇḍala, the most recent, once in the first and once in the ninth, in the sense of a horde, sometimes figuratively, as in the case of dice, but often in the sense of a collection of men in an indefinite number. The word is thrice contrasted,[2] so to say, with *Gaṇa* connoting a definite number and once with Sardha, an assembly. In the sixth maṇḍala[3], the word is undoubtedly used in the sense of an inimical horde. In describing the armoury in the chariot, the poet says, it should be *vrāta-sahā*, capable of resisting the horde; and the sixth maṇḍala is attributed to the family of Ṛṣi Bharadvāja. In the third[4] attributed to Viśvāmitra and in the fifth[5] attributed to Ātreya, the word undoubtedly means a horde, but may mean an enemy horde also. In the first maṇḍala,[6] the horse is said to be followed by chariots, men, women, and *vrātas* as opposed to men. The ninth[7] speaks of five hordes. In two passages in the tenth[8] it is figuratively used for dice and the other contains a sentence—"we will join the vrātas."[9] The oldest use of *vrāta* is in the sense of an inimical horde. Other passages are not opposed to this sense. In the Atharva-

---

[1] Manu II. 39 and X. 20. [2] III. 26. 6 ; V. 53. 11 ; X 34, 12. [3] VI. 75. 9.
[4] III. 26. 6. [5] V. 53. 11. [6] I. 163, 8.
[7] IX. 14, 2. [8] X. 34, 8 ; X 34, 12. [9] X. 57, 5.

Veda[1] too, the word is used in the same sense. In the Vājasaneya and Taittirīya Saṃhitās, in the chapter on Rudra, Vrātapati is used along with *vrāta*.[2] European scholars think that Vrātapati there means the head of a robber band. This also means an inimical horde. So the word means a horde and an inimical horde. They had their temporary settlements, for in the Pañchaviṁśa Brāhmaṇa, they are said to sojourn in *vrātyā* (*vrātyām pravasantaḥ*,[3] where pra-vas means a sojourn) and they had their patriarchs (Gṛhapati), and one of their Gṛhapatis when purified became the founder of a Śākhā of the Ṛg-Veda. But of this later on. They had no Brahmanic culture (Brahmacharya), no agriculture and no trade.[4] All this stamps them as nomad hordes. Those who form the *vrāta*, those who join the *vrāta* and those who are stolen to the *vrāta* are all *vrātyas*. The Māgadhas are friends, intimates, cronies and loud praisers of the Vrātyas.[5] So they must be living in the same country or in close proximity.

To what stock did the Vrātyas belong? The answer is given in the Pañchaviṁśa Brāhmaṇa.[6] They were Daiva prajā, worshippers and favourites of gods—the same gods as were worshipped by the Vedic Aryans. What was the difference then? The gods of the Vrātyas went to Heaven and Vrātyas became dispirited. They lived in their temporary sojourn. They came to the place whence the gods went to heaven. But they did not know the chant and the metre by which they could be united with their gods. Maruts gave them the chant and the metre and so they rejoined their gods. This shows that they worshipped

[1] II. 9, 2. [2] Vāj XVI. 25. Tait IV. 5. 4. 1. [3] XVII. 1. 5. 12.
[4] XVII. 1. 2. [5] Av. XV. [6] XVII. 1.

the same gods as the Vedic Aryans did and on purification they were admitted in the Vedic society on equal terms.

But the peculiar ceremony of the purification of the Vrātyas is performed by a large number of the Vrātyas[1] as yajmānas. The man among them who supplied the *yūpa* and *añjana* and uttered the *Ṛtuyājyā* was said to have been their Gṛhapati or patriarch.[2] Before purification the Vrātyas were sinful[3], inasmuch as they forcibly ate the food prepared in fixed Aryan settlements for the use of sacrificers. They found fault with refined speech, they punished with death innocent people, and though uninitiated they talked like the initiated. These were the four sins to their credit and all these could be dispelled only by four times repeating the sixteen *stomas*. One of the sāmans in these *stomas* is the Dyautāna Sāman[5] in honour of the Maruts. This is the most auspicious Sāman as Dyutāna, the worshipper of the Maruts was the Gṛhapati of the Vrātyas, and he it was who saw this Sāman.

The Pañchaviṃśa Brāhmaṇa names another Gṛhapati of the Vrātyas. He was no other than Kauṣītaka,[6] the son of Samaśravaḥ. He was an old Vrātya who lost his virility. He performed the Vrātyastoma with others, but there was some defect in the arrangement of the stomas and so Lusākapi, the son of Khargala cursed him saying that Kauṣītakīs will not prosper. Sāyana says the Kauṣītaka is the seer of one of the sākhās of Ṛg.-Veda. If a Vrātya imperfectly purified could be the founder of

---

[1] Tandya VI. 9, 24 and XVII. 1. 7. Comm.
[2] XVII. 1. 7. Comm.
[3] XVII. 1. 9.
[4] XVII. 1. 7.
[5] 5 XII. 1. 7.
[6] Tandya 17, 4, 3 and Comm.

a Sākhā of the Rg.-Veda, the Vrātyas could not possibly belong to any other stock than the Vedic Aryans.

Now the question arises, Are the Vrātyas the earlier stock or are they seceders from the Vedic stock? Of course, there were some seceders as the nomads are notoriously child-lifters and man-lifters. But probably they were the earlier stock, the people of the first migration, as Sir George Grierson will say,—those who overran the greater part of the Āryāvarta and left their stamp on the languages of Bengal and Western Punjab alike, but not in the centre of this vast territory, which was occupied by the second and subsequent migration.

This is evidenced by the fact that the Vrātya Chapter *i.e*, the 15th Chapter of the Atharva Veda speaks of an Antardesa from which the Vrātya goes to the East, to the West, to the North, to the South and to the Upper Regions and to the Fixed Regions. He also goes to the Antardeśa. So he is everywhere. The quarters protected him and gave him servitors. The East gave him *Bhava*, the South *Sarva*, the West *Paśupati*, the North *Ugra*, Dhruva (the fixed region) *Rudra*, the Upper *Mahādeva*, and the *Antardeśa*, *Īśāna*. He was himself *Ekavrātya*, *Mahādeva* and *Īśāna*. Now all these Devas mentioned here are daily worshipped by every Brāhmaṇa as different forms of *Śiva*. If this *Ekavrātya* be our *Śiva*, he would not be admitted into the Vedic Pantheon without a struggle and that struggle would be the struggle of *Dakṣa-Yajña*. This is also to some extent foreshadowed in one of the statements in this Chapter, *viz*, that if the Vrātya goes as a guest to a Brāhmaṇ's house when the

[1] Since writing this I received Sir G. Grierson's Index of language names and I find that the Brajabhāsā is still called Antardeśī p. 36. This leaves no doubt as regards the position of Antardeśa.

Brāhmaṇa is engaged in a sacrifice, he should at once rise up and ask the Vrātya to perform the sacrifice himself. On his declining, he should ask the Vrātya's permission to perform it himself; if he permits the sacrifice should be finished; if not, it should not be performed and if performed without his permission, the performer instead of acquiring virtue shall incur sin. This is a digression, but I could not resist the temptation of the digression, it is so fascinating.

So the Vrātyas were everywhere,—on all sides of the *Antardeśa* and also within the *Antardeśa.* But the east seems to be their principal resort, for in the *Pañchaviṃśa Brāhmaṇa* there is an obscure passage, made still more obscure by Sāyana's interpretation—*Kakubhaṃ prāchīm anuvyachalat* ("went to the Eastern Quarter"). In the Atharva Veda the order of the quarters begins always with Prāchī and the quarters have their bearing from *Antardeśa.*

The Vrātyas differed in many ways from the Vedic Aryans. Their headdress was worn in a slanting fashion[1] while that of the Aryans was not so. They had a bow without string; incapable, as Kātyāyaṇa explains, of throwing arrows. The bow was perhaps used as a club as some people still do. In the Atharva-Veda the rainbow is the bow of the *Ekavrātya* without string. Its concave side was red and its convex side blue; with the red side he covered his enemies and with the blue side he pierced his antagonist. But not so the bow of the Vedic Aryans. It had a string and it threw arrows. The Vrātyas used rough carts, covered with loose planks, which often went out of the road; while the Vedic

---

[1] Tāṇḍya XVII, 1. 14. 15. Kātya XXII. 132ff. Lātyvāyana VIII. 6ff.

Aryan had chariots furnished with a strong armoury capable of holding a number of arrows, and the draught animal, horse or bullock, restrained by reins. The horses and mules of the Vrātyas drawing chariots were *kampra* lit. "shaky," unrestrained ; while the Vedic Aryans restrained their horses with reins. The animals of the Vrātyas went out of the road. The Vedic Aryans had reins but the Vrātyas had *pratoda* (a stick with a string of leather attached, still used in driving bullock-carts). The cloth used by the Vrātyas had black border crosswise, while Brahmins are still prohibited to use such borders. They had two pieces of sheep-skin bordered with white embroidery, while there was no such border with the others. These had silver ornaments while the other had ornaments of gold.

The above mentioned articles were used by the higher classes of the Vrātyas, their *Gṛhapatis* (Patriarchs), while the ordinary people used cloth with red borders and with strings at the other end. They used two sandals of black skin with ears and two sheep skins. This differs greatly from the dress of the Vedic Aryans.

After purification the possessions of the Vrātyas were to be given away to the Vrātyas, those who still remain in their *vrātyās* or to the so-called Brahmins of the Magadha country. Kātyāyana says the latter are to be preferred. After the fees are paid to the Ṛtviks, the purified Vrātya may acquire knowledge of the three Vedas and may be admitted to society. His food may be taken and he may be taught the sacred lore.

The long disquisition has some bearing on our subject. The *vipatha* or "rough cart" of the Vrātya is called by Lātyāyana *Prāchyaratha* or 'Eastern Chariot' and their property is to be given to the Brahmanas of Magadha. So the Vrātyas are in many ways connected with Magadha.

2

They were the Aryans of the first migration in nomadic hordes. They were simpler and more primitive in their habits and mode of living and with a short purificatory ceremony they were fully admitted into the Vedic society.

The Vrātyas were certainly not confined to the East but they were in every direction, as the Atharva-Veda distinctly says. But in the north, their expansion was limited by the Himalayas, in the south by the Vindhyas and in the West by the pressure of other tribes, while in the East they had almost unlimited scope for expansion. They made the original inhabitants, or the upper classes among them, their friends and advisers, and lived on patches of plains cleared of jungles in their temporary habitations with their horses and cattle. Loot also they indulged in and man-lifting and cattle-lifting.

There were another people, the *Vrātinas*, the priests for the cruel rite of *Śyena-Yāga* This word *Vrātina* is undoubtedly derived from the same word *Vrāta* a nomad horde inimical to the Aryans. They had their learning and they had their warriors. If the warrior's son is a learned man, he should be preferred as a priest for this cruel rite. Here the commentator raises a question and a vital question too. How can a man not born in the family of a Ṛṣi perform a sacrifice? and comes to the conclusion that for this particular ceremony a descent from a Ṛṣi is not absolutely necessary. But he should have learning, though not the learning of a Vedic Aryan. The place for the ceremony is a recent clearance in the midst of a jungle. Thick trees and trunks should be cut for the purpose. The planks for the purpose of pressing juice should be the planks of ambulance carts for carrying away dead bodies. The priest should wear a red head-dress and red cloth, look fierce and have his bow strung. One of the authors, Sāṇḍilya, says that Arhats should be made priests in this cruel rite. Now the word "Arhat" is significant. The word was in use in Pre-Buddhistic days in the sense of worthy, wise men, medicine men, wizards, etc , as in all primitive socities. So it was adopted by the Buddhists and the Jainas, and it came to mean monks of their sects.

So there were *Vrātyas* and *Vrātinas*, both nomad hordes not within the pale of the Vedic Aryan Society, claiming no descent from Ṛṣis, having priests of their own, performing primitive rites according to their own ideas. These, the Vedic Aryans were anxious to bring to their own fold. There are various indications that the majority of the nomads were roaming in the East,—east of the Aryan land of the Vedas.

Thus we have in the Vedic literature the Magadhas the name of a tribe, Magadha, the name of the country inhabited by Magadhas, Māgadhas, inhabitants of the Magadha country not belonging to the Magadha tribe. The country was not in good repute with the Vedic people. A Brahmin living in the Magadha country was called a *Brahmabandhu*—a so-called Brahmin—a bad Brahmin. Even in the Purāṇas, the Śiśunāgas were called *Kṣattrabandhus* or bad Kṣattriyas. The Kauśítakis alone were favourably disposed to the country and say in their Āraṇyaka that *Madhyamaprātibodhiputra* lived in Magadha country, but was a very respectable Brahmin So the country was a non-Aryan country, then came the Vrātyas, the Aryans of the first migration, and they came to stay. They made friends with the Māgadhas and became very influential; and the Vedic Aryans, the Aryans of the second migration tried hard to bring them to their own fold. This is all that we can glean from the scanty information vouchsafed to us by the Vedic literature.

Magadha is better known in the classical literature. But before entering into that literature it is necessary to know what time elapsed between the close of the Vedic and the commencement of the Classical literature. Max Müller in his History of Ancient Sanskrit Literature written in 1859 limited the Sūtra literature between 600-200 B. C. But Bühler in page xxii of his Introduction to his translation of the *Mānava-Dharma-Śāstra* in the S. B E. Series (1886) says, "It seems no longer advisable to limit the production of Sūtras to so short and so late a period as 600-200 B C." But works have been discovered, facts brought to light and interpretation put on old materials which seem to justify the inference that the Sūtra activity of the Vedic *Charaṇas* closed sometime before the advent of Buddha and his contemporary reformers, *i.e.*, the higher limit of Max Müller may be the lower limit of these activities. For he seems to have included the activity of the special schools within this period which Bühler pronounced to be short and late. The Sūtras of the Vedic School seem to have been followed by a long period in which many comprehensive Sūtra works of special schools were written. The aphoristic form of writing continued, but not of the Vedic Schools. The fall of Taxila into the hands of the Persians seems to have dealt a death blow to the Vedic Sūtra activities, and the transference of the intellectual capital of India from Taxila to Pāṭaliputra gave an impetus to the Sūtra activity of another sort. Already the tendency in Taxila seems to have been to write comprehensive works in Sūtra form, but at Pāṭaliputra, the rulers of which were aiming at Imperial dominion, that tendency was encourag-

---

[1] Lâtyāyana VIII 5.

ed, fostered and taken special care of; and it bore rich and exhuberant fruits.

The activity was not confined to the six *aṅgas* of the Vedas but it spread over various other branches of knowledge, such as Medicine, economics, politics, history, philosophy, science, dramaturgy and even erotics. The aphoristic style at last proved to be too terse and too enigmatic and some of the writers began to give their own comments to elucidate the aphorisms, and then they hit upon the plan of writing long metrical works to make the subjects more attractive and easier to commit to memory—the only method of imparting and receiving instructions in those days—and easier to apply them to practical purposes of life. Max Müller thinks that the long versified works in śloka metre came into existence at the close of the sūtra period about 200 B. C. But Bühler has shown that they existed some centuries earlier.

This is a digression, but a digression necessary to understand the condition of India and specially of Magadha, during the classical period of aphorisms and śloka metre. During the period, Western India, the *Antardeśa* of the Atharva-Veda, was under the sway of Brahmanical institutions with their small political units with their complicated sacrificial rites, with constant and long isolated parochial ideas, with their class-interest and with their narrow views. They still remained spell bound by their old tradition which they found difficult to break through. But not so in the East, where though the Brahmin influence was paramount, there were other elements which developed in other directions The number of Brahmins were few compared to that of *Antardeśa*. The majority of Aryan people were Vrātyas, or recently converted Vrātyas, the tribe of Magadhas and Māgadhas, the most vigorous of these being the Vrātyas in two sections. They had no Brahmanical discipline, no agriculture and no commerce during the Vedic period. But within a short time after their conversion, they had wonderfully developed their trade and their national wealth. They had freedom to develop their own institutions, civil and military, and they had also caught something like Imperialistic idea. The Śākyas and Mallas in Northern Oudh, Lichhavis and Videhas in North Bihar, the Aṅgas in the East, the Kāśis on the West and the Bārhadrathas in the centre, *i e*, Magadha,—all became prosperous states with cities teeming with busy population, country sites rolling in plenty, rivers covered over with crafts full of merchandise, with Assembly-halls ringing with speeches, songs, plays, discussions and disputations, with horses and elephants in plenty, with splendid processions and imposing pageants. Brahmins were their teachers, keepers of their conscience, the priests in their temples and *ṛtviks* in their sacrifices. But the young vigorous people soon outgrew the influence of their teachers and began to think for themselves. The mighty upheaval of intellectual, moral and political life in the 6th and 7th centuries before Christ was the result of their comparative freedom from the thraldom of the Brahmins, of the rise of monastic life in their midst and of the transference of the intellectual capital from Taxilla to Pāṭaliputra The system of the four castes. with their numerous crosses sat rather loose on them. The *Antardeśa* however, showed a different spectacle Various foreign races, flying from invading hordes, sought refuge amongst them and disturbed the quiet prosperity of their land. The *Suberas* driven away from Chaldea by the Semites settled at Sindh. The Medés driven from their home by the Persians came to settle in their country. And last of all, the Persians came and occupied its most prosperous parts. The *Antardeśa* which was already much weakened by internal dissensions as revealed in the Purāṇas contrasted very unfavourably with the prosperous east, which the dispoiled westerners sought for a safe refuge. This greatly added to the prosperity of that country.

Just at this psychological moment, the Bārhadrathas were overthrown by a new and vigorous race, the Śiśunāgas who were characterised as *Kṣatrabandhavah* i.e., "so-called Kṣattriyas," meaning no doubt that they were Vrātyas, on whom the Brahminic institutions did not sit very tight. But they conformed to all that the Brahmins said. They were mostly converted into Kṣatriyas, and had to give up some of their nomadic habits. The dress of the Śiśunāga statues conforms wonderfully to the dress described by Lātyāyana, Kātyāyana and others as proper for a Vrātya.

It would not be out of place to mention here that since Vedic times, the conception of Vrātyas considerably changed. In the Vedic literature they were a nomad horde without Brahmins, without a caste system, without a fixed residence and without a settled Government. They were a patriarchal people, moving with their flocks from one place to another. But in the classical literature the Vrātyas were regarded as a Brahminic people divided into the first three castes, but without Brahminical sacraments. It was thought by some that they were descended from men of these three castes on their own caste women, but that they did not take their sacraments. Another authority says that sons begotten by people without sacraments on their own caste women, were the Vrātyas So the Brahmins seem to have imposed some sort of caste system on them during the interval. In the Vedas the Vrātyas formed only one class, while in the classical period there were Brahmin Vrātyas, Kṣattriya

Vrātyas and Vaiśya Vrātyas. Curiously enough, the Brahmin Vrātyas were to be found on all sides of *Antardeśa*, but the east, where there were only Kṣattriya Vrātyas. This is as it should be. Because the number of the Vrātyas was very very large on the east as I had shown before. In this matter I will adduce the evidence of three works, the earliest being that of the *Lalita Vistara*, which though reduced to its present shape in later centuries, embodies the traditions of the 5th or 6th centuries B. C. Then of the Arthaśāstra written in the latter end of the 4th century, and of the *Mānava-Dharma-Śāstra* reduced in its present shape during the ascendency of the Brahmins of the Śunga Dynasty.

The Buddha when surveying this world from the *Tuṣita-Bhuvana* for his last birth, passed in review all the countries then known.[1] The border countries were not acceptable to him. The Madhyama, the Middle country of Yuan Chwang—had then sixteen states. Of these eight were described and rejected—*Pradyotanapura* (Ujjain), (2) *Mathurā*, (3) *Hastināpura*, (4) *Vanisa* (perhaps *Vatsa*), (5) *Kośala*, (6) *Videha*, (7) *Mithilá* and (8) *Vaiśáli*. The last was rejected because there was no king, and everyone thought he was supreme. Hastinā was rejected for the same reason. Others were rejected for other reasons. It was at last settled that he should be born in a Kṣattriya family; for the world is no longer governed by the Brahmins but by Kṣattriyas, and at last, the Śākya family was selected for his birth.[1]

In the Arthaśāstra[2] of Kauṭilya we find that Kāmboja and Saurāṣṭra were inhabited by tribes (Śreṇī) of Kṣattriyas who lived by agriculture, trade and by the profession of

---

1 Lalitavistara Bible, Ind. Ed. p. 22 ff.

2 Artha Sastra Mysore Ed. I p. 326ff.

arms. The Licchavis, the Vṛjjis, the Mallas, the Madras, the Kukuras, the Kurus and the Pāñchālas lived by the title of Rājā. Living by the title of Rājā may seem to be strange. But there is a discussion in the Śavara-Bhāṣya on the word Rājā which is likely to throw much light on its meaning. The word "Rājā" there is said to mean anyone engaged in the work of a Rājā, royal officer, or engaged in the work of Government. It may or may not necessarily mean a Kṣattriya, for the Bhāṣya says that in the Andhra country the Rājās or the governing classes are not always Kṣattriyas. So the Licchavis and others mentioned in the Arthaśāstra may or may not be Kṣattriyas, for Vaijayantī, a Buddhist work distinctly says that the Licchavis were Vrātya-Kṣattriyas.

Manava-Dharma-Śāstra on the other hand classified the Vrātyas in three Varṇas, Brāhmins, Kṣattriyas and Vaiśyas For it says that the Vrātya Brāhmins were Āvantyas living in the south-west, Bāṭadhānas in the north-west, the Bhṛijyakaṇṭakas and the Puṣpaśekharas. The abode of these latter is not known. But Bühler says, they were spies and sorcerers. The Vrātya-Kṣattriyas were the Jhallas, the Mallas, the Licchavis, the Naṭas, the Karaṇas, the Khaśas and the Draviḍas. Of them, the Mallas and Licchavis certainly belong to the east. The Vrātyas Vaiśya were Sudhanvā, Āchāryya, Kāruṣa, Vijanma, Maitra and Satata. We know nothing about the place of abode and the occupation of the Vrātya Vaiśyas

Though the commentators of the Manava-Dharma-Śāstra say that there were something like castes, some living by espionage, some by worshipping images of gods, some as temple priests, some by drawing water and some by other means, Bühler thinks that "it is very probable that all these names originally denoted nations"

3

and he seems to be right as they all seem to have been outside the pale of Vedic Aryan Society. I know that Ächāryyas are still temple-priests to the lower order of Hindus in Nepal. Kāruṣas, it is well-known gave their name to the country between Kośala and Videha.

From the statements of these three great authorities it seems that the country east of the Aryan land was inhabited by Vrātyas, nations who were imperfectly Brahminized. They were all fighting races, or races engaged in subduing and keeping under control the aboriginal people, Magadhas, Māgadhas and others; and they lived like princes on the produce of the land cultivated by their subject people. They were all rājās and so were admitted into the caste system by Vedic Brahmins in their works. They were most probably the Rājanyas who like the modern Rājputs were called Kṣattriyas by Brahmin writers from interested or political motives.

Mahāgovinda-Sutra, the most ancient authority on the Buddhist side, on the political geography of India, both in its Pali version and in the mixed Sanskrit version (i.e. Mahāvastu) states that Magadha was a dependent of the Aṅga country and that Kośala was dependent on Kāśī. But we find in Buddha's time Aṇga was a state dependent on Magadha, and Kāśī on Kośala. This change of status was brought about most likely by the advent of the Śiśunāgas, Kṣattrabāndhavas or Vrātya race, one or two generations before the birth of Buddha during whose life-time the kings of Magadha and Kośala were fighting for the supremacy in the east, with the confederacy of the Śākyas, Mallas, Licchavis, Vṛjjis, Videhas and others occupying the territory north of Magadha and east of Kośala The Kurus, the Pāñchālas, the Madras were also at this time confederacies and there is a book and an entire book in the Arthaśāstra dealing with these confederate people entitled *Sangha-Vrittam.*

Some centuries before the Buddha appeared on the scene, Taxila was the centre of Vedic civilization. It was here that Janamejaya performed his famous Serpent-sacrifice ; it was here that Mahābhārata was first recited ; it was here that a beginning was made of the classical literature ; it was here that people flocked from all parts of civilized India to finish their education ; and it was here that all Indian sciences had their origin. Jīvaka, the earliest medical man known belongs to Taxila. The earliest grammarian known belongs to that city. The earliest writer of Mimāusa too, belongs to that city. The earliest writer on Veterinary science on horse, belongs to its vicinity In fact, all works in classical Sanskrit apart from works written in the interest of Vedic Schools in their Pariṣads, all seem to have their origin in Taxila.

But a great calamity overtook Taxila during the life-time of Buddha. It was conquered by Darius, the Persian monarch who destroyed the dynasty founded by Cyrus, and kept a considerable portion of the North-Western India for a century under his control. Taxila lost its high position as the centre of learning, compelling eminent scholars like Panini, Varsa and Upavarsa to seek the eastern region as a field of work. Pātaliputra was then fast rising into fame as the capital of the most powerful kingdom in the east ; and they came there and were honoured by the king in their quinquennial assemblies in a manner befitting their learning and their position in society. Thus began the literature of Magadha, long after Vedic Sanskrit had ceased to be the language of the Brahmins. It was obsolescent, but not yet absolutely obsolete. At Taxila, Indian learning had very nearly shaken off the narrow groove in which the Vedic schools moved, but at Pataliputra it assumed a universal, nay even an Imperialistic character.

When the Vedic Literature came to an end and the art of writing was either invented or introduced, the language of the Aryans was in chaos. Some stood for the dictionaries and idioms of the Vedic schools, others for phonetically softened expressions of the vernaculars. Dialects vary in every district—the dialects both of the higher classes, and the lower putting very great obstacles to free and unrestricted intercourse between one district and another. The disadvantages were great, specially of the higher classes who had a good deal of travel to undertake. This led to the origin of classical Sanskrit or simply Sanskrit language—the language purified from all vernacular taints and irregularities. This necessitated writing of grammars other than Vedic school grammars. There were fifteen or sixteen such grammars of classical language before Pāṇini undertook to survey the whole field of the language of the cultured classes; and his two successors gave it such a character and immutability that it lasts even to the present day. The vernaculars again, developed, each in its own district and the religious reformers of the 6th century B. C. gave many of them, a shape and a literature. Some again, wanted to interpret the classical ideas to the common folk and used a mixed language, which is neither Sanskrit nor vernacular, but a mixture of both. I believe that the dramas were originally written in this mixed language, in order that they might be enjoyed both by the higher and the lower classes alike. The reason for my belief is a statement in Daṇḍin's *Kavyādarśa*,[1] that there are four varieties of the language of India, namely Saṁskrita, Prākrita, Apabhraṁśa and Miśra. For

---

[1] Kavyadarsa I 32ff.

Miśra he gives the example,—"of dramas and others." We have not as yet been able to lay our hands upon a drama written purely in the mixed language. In the dramas that are extant, some people speak Sanskrit and some Prakrit. Hence the commentators interpret the statement *Naṭakādi tu Miśrakaṃ* as meaning Nāṭaka in Sanskrit and Prakrit. But they forget that Daṇḍin was in that enumeration giving an example of language and not of a form of literature. The discovery of a considerable body of literature and of a large number of inscriptions in the mixed language confirms me in my belief.

So in dealing with Magadhan Literature, one has not only to think of Sanskrit classical literature, but also of Prakrit literature in its variety of forms, and also of literature in the mixed language. Literature in Classical Sanskrit is wholly Brahminic in the Magadha Empire, and literature in Prakrit belongs to the Reformed schools. The literature in mixed language was the result of putting the ideas of the Reformed schools in Brahminic shape.

So you can see the magnitude of the work I have undertaken to deal with. It includes a vast number of Sanskrit works, the whole of ancient Buddhist Literature and the whole of the ancient Jaina literature. But fortunately for me, the literature of the Buddhists and the Jainas have so often been revised and re-revised, translated and retranslated in the languages of subsequent centuries that they may be considered to have lost their Magadhan character.

THE SEVEN GREAT WRITERS.

Lecture II.

In my first lecture some idea has been given as to who the inhabitants of Magadha were, and as to the languages that were current there at the commencement of the rule of the Sīsunāgas. Now it is time, that its literature should be dealt with. Time has not yet come, researches in literature have not yet sufficiently advanced, for writing a complete and comprehensive literary history of the Magadha empire. But the subject is so interesting and so fascinating that any attempt however partial and imperfect, is likely to be welcome to scholars. When the materials are admittedly so scanty, it would be rash to attempt a chronological statement. So the following pages will be devoted to an endeavour to piece together, from such information as are available, materials which are likely to throw some light on the literary history of Magadha, and at the same time to be attractive to the general reader.

The Bārhadratha Dynasty ended, and Sīsunāga became the king of Magadha in the beginning of the 7th century B. C. The Sīsunāgas are described as Kṣattriyabandhus *i.e.* so called Ksattriyas. Buddha was born in the reign of Bimbisāra. His son Ajātasatru founded the city of Pātaliputra. Udayī, his grandson transferred the capital from Rājagṛiha to Pāṭaliputra. Just at this time Taxila, the centre of Brahmanic learning, languished under foreign dominion; and the great scholars there began to resort to the eastern capital. Thus we have a tradition in Rājaśekhara's Kāvya Mīmāmsā in the following words :—

श्रूयते च पाटलिपुत्रे शास्त्रकारपरीक्षा—
अत्रोपवर्षवर्षाविह पाणिनिपिंगलाविह व्याडिः ।
वररुचिपतंजली इह परीक्षिताः ख्यातिमुपजग्मुः ॥[1]

"The tradition of the examination of the authors of Śāstras at Pātaliputra runs thus :—Here Upavarṣa and Varṣa, here Paṇini and Piṅgala, here Vyāḍi and here Bararuci and Patañjali having been examined rose to fame."

The most noteworthy word in this tradition is Śāstrakāra. All through ancient literature, Hindu or Budhist, the distinction between the Sūtra and Śāstra is, though not very rigidly, always maintained. So the literature of Magadha begins not with Sūtra, but with Śāstra ; that shows that the old Sūtra period was at an end, the Sūtras of Vedic School were now out of fashion, and that their place had been taken by comprehensive works called Śāstras though still written in Sūtra style—the current style of the literature of the time. In the above list of scholars the name of Upavarṣa stands first and foremost, and I believe, first also in chronological order. Upavarṣa was a Mīmāṃsā writer.[2] His works have all been lost. He is sometimes called a Sūtrakāra or sometimes a Vrittikāra. Kṛishṇadeva in his Tantra Chūḍāmaṇi, a Mīmāṃsā work says that a Vṛitti was composed on the Mīmāṃsā Sūtras by Upavarṣa. The Catalogus Catalogorum on the other hand states, on the authority of Bhāskara-Miśra, that there was a Sūtrakāra named Upavarṣa. Whoever he might have been, a Sūtrakāra or

[1] Kāvya mīmaṃśā p. 55.

[2] Hall's contributions mīmāṃsa

a Vrittikāra, he came to Pāṭaliputra and was honoured by its King. The Mīmāṃsā as a system of interpretation of the Vedic injunctions, found in the Brāhmaṇas, and systematized for practical purposes in the Kalpa-Sūtras, existed from remote antiquity. It went by a variety of names Mīmāṃsā, Nyāya, Naya and others. Gautama-Dharma-Śāstra one of the oldest Sūtras on Dharma speaks of Mīmāṃsā. In the Pratimā-Nātaka, Rāvaṇa speaks to Sītā of his study of Mīmāṃsā (Nyāya-Śāstra) from Medhātithi.

It may be asked here why is it that while Pāṇini's Grammar and Pingala's Chanda suppressed all old grammars and Chanda works attached to different Śākhās, Mīmāṃsā did not succeed in suppressing the older Kalpa-Sūtras of the Vedic Schools. The Sūtras served a practical purpose. They settled the details of sacrifices, while the Mīmāṃsā dealt only with the general principles thereof, as well as the laws of interpretation. The Mīmāṃsā served as a corrector of the Kalpa-Sūtras and their practices, and so it could not suppress them.

There is a long quotation in the first chapter of the first pāda of the Śavara-Bhāṣya written in an ancient style which Kṛṣṇadeva attributed to Upavarṣa. Śavara-Bhāṣya must have been written after the rise of Mahāyāna. For it distinctly says—

अनेन प्रत्युक्तो महायानिकः पक्षाः ।

"Thus are refuted the arguments of the Mahāyānists." The editor of the Bhāṣya, 50 years ago, not knowing the word Mahāyānika changed it into Mahājānika, deriving it from Mahājana, though all his manuscripts read 'Mahāyānika.' So Upavarṣa must have been regarded as an ancient authority when Śavara wrote. But Śavara only says Vṛittikāra and not Upavarṣa. It is

4

extremely difficult to decide what work was written by Upavarṣa, a Śāstra in Sūtra form, or a Vṛtti, most probably the former, for his companions in the traditional verse are all Śāstrakāras, original writers.

There is reason to believe that the list is chronological. For it will be shown later on, that the people of Magadha, with whom evidently the tradition originated, had a good historical sense, and a sound chronological idea. There is a grammatical reason too, for believing the list to be chronological. Ordinarily the copulative compound should be Varṣopavarṣau, the shorter word coming first. But here it is Upavarṣavarṣau for the special reason of Upavarṣa's being *Abhyarhita* or more venerable *i.e.*, more ancient. Moreover, the names which follow, are all in strictly chronological order. The second name is that of Varṣa, the teacher of Pāṇini. Third Pāṇini himself. The fourth is Piṅgala, a contemporary of Chandragupta and Bindusāra. The fifth is Vyāḍi who wrote a Saṁgraha or a comprehensive work on all about words. The sixth and seventh are the writers of Vārttika and Bhāṣya on Pāṇini.

Of Varṣa we know nothing except a tradition in Kathā-Saritsāgara that he was the Guru of Pāṇini, and so he must have come from Taxila or its suburbs as Pāṇini himself.

Pāṇini was an inhabitant of Śālātura, a suburb of Taxila. His statue is referred to by Yuan Chwang as having been in existence at Śālātura long before his time. His age was a subject of fierce controversy for nearly a century. Professor Goldstücker would place him immediately after the compilation of the Ṛk, Yajus and Sāma Vedas and the composition of Yāska's Nirukta. Bühler with great caution has placed him in 375 B. C. on the evidence Katha-Saritsāgara. Pandit Satyavrata

Sāmaśramī would like to place him before Yāska. But none of them seem to have been aware of the tradition in Kāvya Mīmāṁsā. It is a curious thing, however, as will be shown later on, that Kauṭilya seems not to know Pāṇini. Kauṭilya when speaking of Grammar, speaks of 63 letters and four parts of speech; while the number of letters in Pāṇini is 64 and his parts of speech are only two. Pāṇini classifies all the words in the language into Subanta and Tiṅanta. He is so very anxious for a non-overlapping complete division by dichotomy that he includes the Avyayas or indeclinable particles which take no grammatical termination, into Subanta and makes them drop their case endings. Some one may say that that is ultra-scientific, but it is strictly logical, although unpractical and difficult for beginners to comprehend. The older school had a fourfold divison of words, namely, Nāman (noun), Ākhyāta (verb), Upasarga (prefixes) and Nipāta (particles). To this later on, perhaps in the seventh century, Helārāja, the commentator of Bhartṛhari's Vākyapadīya, added a fifth, Karma-pravacanīya or "post-positions" governing cases. something like English prepositions. Rājaśekhara followed Helārāja. Sāyana in his commentary on Taittiriya Brāhmaṇa says that the four fold division is Śrauta, though opposed to Pāṇini; and the fact that Yāska adopts the four-fold division lends support to Sayana's views. The non-adoption of Pāṇinean system by Kauṭilya argues that Pāṇini had not yet taken deep root, and that he was not regarded as an ancient and sacred authority.

Pāṇini is divided into eight books of four sections each, there being altogether 3983 sūtras. According to Bhaṭṭojī Dīkṣita's calculation, they are 3978; and according to Professor Goldstücker's they are 3993. In the handy edition of Siddhānta-Kaumudī, published in Bombay in

Śaka 1815 by Kāśīnatha Parava, is given a Sūtrapātha of Pāṇini. At the end of each pāda of the edition are given the pratīka of groups of 20 sūtras and the pratīkas of the last group which falls short of 20. It is by counting these that I have arrived at the figure 3983; and I have checked it by Jīvānanda's edition of Sūtrapātha; and I find Burnell also arrived at the same figure. Arrangement of sūtras in comparatively modern Sanskrit grammars is made to serve a practical purpose, namely, to teach the forms of language, so that students may learn something of the language as they proceed. But such is the arrangement of Pāṇini that nobody can apply his work to the language without studying the whole of the sūtras. Other grammars, so to say, are school-books; while Pāṇini's is a scientific work on Philology of the highest value. His work is based on a number of previous works on the subject. The authors to whom he is indebted are:—Āpiśali, Kāśyapa, Gārgya, Gālava, Chakravarman, Bhāradvāja, Śākaṭāyana Śākalya, Senaka and Sphoṭāyana. There are other grammarians who are quoted by him as northern and eastern. Sometimes he refers to Ācharyya in the plural, meaning perhaps his own Guru, Varṣa.

As regards the age of Pāṇini, Goldstücker says, "We have seen that within the whole range of Sanskrit Literature so far as is known to us, the Saṃhitās of Ṛk, Sāman and Black Yajur-Veda and among individual authors the exegete Yāska preceded Pāṇini—that the whole bulk of the remaining literature is posterior to the eight grammatical books." Therefore, Pāṇini must be very ancient. The entire Brāhmaṇa literature was written after him; all the Āraṇyakas, Upaniṣads and Kalpa-Sūtras are post-Paṇinean. But Goldstücker's premises are not all correct. Pāṇini writes sūtras for the Brāhmaṇa Literature. In II, iii, 60 he gives a rule for Brāhmaṇas only. He has many rules for mantras only (II, iv, 80; III, ii, 71 VI, i, 151; VI, iv, 53), one for Yajus only (VIII, iii, 104), and two for Yajña (VIII, ii, 88; VI, iv, 54). So the statement made in general that Pāṇini knew only the three Saṁhitās and no Brāhmaṇas cannot be maintained. He makes rules for Mantras and Yajus as distinct from Chandas. That also shows that the majority of his Vedic rules refers to the Brāhmaṇa literature also, because many mantras are to be found in the Brāhmaṇas, for instance, the Mantra-Brāhmaṇa of the Sāma Veda. It is also evident from IV, iii, 105, and its Vārttika that there were Brāhmaṇas in Pāṇini's time, regarded as ancient and sacred and also as modern, such as Yājñavalkya Brāhmaṇa.

Pāṇini's age cannot be so early in the Vedic Period, as he quotes from so many of his predecessors, grammarians and philologists. Āpiśali wrote on Phonetics. A small fragment of the work by Āpiśali was published 40 years ago. Gārgya and Gālava are quoted also by Yāska. But their books have not come down to us. One work however was published in 1893 from Madras. This is Śākaṭāyana. I believe that it was still recently used by the Jainas of Southern India. The author Śākaṭāyana is there called a Śrutakevalī-deśīyāchāryya. The Śrutakevalī's are the direct disciples of the Tīrthaṃkaras. They became Kevalīs or absolutely emancipated by hearing the doctrine directly from a Tīrthaṃkara. So Śākaṭāyana must have been a younger contemporary of a Tīrthaṃkara. And Patañjali says that he was so absorbed in meditation that while sitting on a chariot road he did not perceive a caravan of chariots passing by. This is just what a Śrutakevalī should be. Of the 24 Tīrthāṃkaras of the Jainas, the last two are regarded as historical, Parsvanātha (who was born at Benares and died at Sametagiri, modern Paresnāth Hills in Hāzāribāgh) and Vardhamāna (who was born at Vaiśāli and died at Pāvā near Rājgir). It is generally understood that two centuries elapsed between the two. Vardhamāna after renouncing the world joined a Jaina monastery at Vaiśālī. Śākaṭāyana seems to have been a Śrutakevalī through Pārśvanātha. For he is quoted not only by Pāṇini but also by Yāska, who must have preceded Pāṇini by several generations, because Yāska's idea of an Upasarga is crude while Pāṇini's is very much advanced and refined. It is not a technical term invented by Pāṇini who takes it from his predecessors and so does not define it. Yāskā's idea of an Upasarga is simply this :—That Upasargas express a variety of senses. But Pāṇini says they are Nipātas or particles; they are Upasargas when joined to verbal actions; gatis, if the verbal roots to which they are attached become nouns; and Karmapravachanīyas when they are detached and govern nouns. Śākaṭāyana on the other hand says that when detached from nouns or verbs they do not distinctly express a sense. So Yāska is in advance of Śākaṭāyana and Pāṇini in advance of Yāska; and this advance must have taken a few generations to develop.

Now, if Śākatāyana is really a Śrutakevalī of Vardhamāna and Pāṇini, the third Śāstrakāra who came to Pāṭaliputra for his reward, there would be no intervening space for Yāska and no sufficient time for developing the idea of Upasargas. Therefore I should think that he was a Śrutakevalī to Pārśvanātha. For he is here not only called a Śrutakevalī, but Śrutakevalī-deśīyāchāryya *i.e.*, an Āchāryya next only to a Śrutakevali. In that case there would be sufficient space of time for the development of the grammatical ideas.

I need not enter here into the discussion as to the genuineness of Śākaṭāyana's grammar as we have it. It is sufficient for my purpose to know that the quotations in Pāṇini from Śākaṭāyana are to be found in this work ; and even Burnell, who tries to show it to be a forgery and a clumsy forgery too, is constrained to admit, " These coincidences prove that our existing treatise is really based on the original work." This is all that I require for my present purpose. I may say in passing that in grammer the room for interpolation and forgery is very limited.

Pāṇini was really a gifted man. His predecessors had a notion that all nouns could be derived from verbal roots. These were called the Vyutpattivādins, and Śākaṭāyana headed the list of Vyutpattivādins. But Pāṇini was opposed to it. He was not a Vyutpattivādin. If the modern system of comparative grammar has taught us anything, it has taught that words borrowed from older stages of a language, cannot be derived from the actual roots in the language itself. Vyutpattivādins have gone so far as to derive from Sanskrit roots even words evidently borrowed from foreign languages.

About the personal history of Pāṇini, we know only this much that he belonged to Śālātura a suburb of Taxila, that his mother's name was Dākṣī, that he was a pupil of Varṣa (and this we know from Katha-Sarit-Sagara and it should be accepted with caution) and that he distinguished himself in a quinquennial assembly held at Pāṭaliputra. There is another piece of information given to us by Patañjali, that he was famous since a boy. This gives a direct lie to the story of Kathā-Sarit-Sagara that he was a dunce in the beginning and that Siva came to his rescue in his disputation with Katyāyana. Patañjali also says that he had a pupil named Kautsa.

As to other works by Pāṇini there is a verse, handed down from remote antiquity, which runs thus :—

अष्टकं गणपाठश्च धातुपाठस्तथैव च ।
लिंगानुशासनं शिक्षा पाणिनीया अमी क्रमात् ॥

Aṣṭakaṃ is Aṣṭādhyāyī *i.e.*, the Sūtrapāṭha. In a large number of sūtras, Gaṇas are mentioned. Gaṇa means a list of words undergoing a common grammatical change. There is a book where all these gaṇas are put together and it is attributed to Pāṇini. But tradition has it that even Śākaṭāyana had a Gaṇapāṭha. The Gaṇas were not made in a day. At the latter end of the Vedic age, professors of various Śākhās carefully indexed all sorts of grammatical peculiarities in their Śākhās. We have a few of these indices such as Padagāḍha, Chaturjñana, Lakṣaṇaratna and so on. These are commonly known as Lakṣaṇagranthas. That these indices helped a great deal in the formation of the sūtras which are simply generalisations from these indices, goes without saying. It was from these that the lists called Gaṇas were drawn; and every grammarian had to make his own lists before compiling his book in Sūtra form. So Pāṇini had also a compilation of Gaṇas.

Similarly every grammarian had to make his own list of verbal roots. Pāṇini's Dhātupaṭha consists of 1944 roots, plus 20 Sauttra dhātus which have to be picked up from the Sūtras of Pāṇini. His Lingānuśāsana consists of 183 sūtras and deals with genders of words. Unlike modern languages Sanskrit has a gender for every noun, not necessarily determined by the sex. The Lingānuśāsana gives rules for determining the genders of nouns.

Pāṇinīya Śikṣā consists of 59 verses in a variety of metres. It gives rules for pronunciation of words, rules for reciting the Vedas and rules for elocution. It begins with a salutation to Pāṇini and Pāṇini is often mentioned in the verses. But in ancient works, authors often speak in the 3rd person as we know from Kauṭilya. The salutations at the beginning and at the end are a later addition. It enumerates letters of the alphabet as 64. It says,—The soul joins intelligence and employs the mind to express objects. The mind strikes the fire in the body and that fire sets the wind in motion. The wind blowing in the chest, produces a deep sound; that in the throat a middling sound; that in the head a shrill sound. That wind striking the head comes to the mouth and produces distinct letters. These letters are divided into five classes: (i) according to pitch, (ii) according to time, (iii) according to the vocal organs, (iv) according to effort and (v) according to touch. The pitches are three, high, low and middling. The time taken may be also short, long or prolonged. Vocal organs are eight, nose, chest, throat, head, root of the tongue, teeth, lips and palate. The efforts are, opening the mouth, shutting, half opening and slight opening. The touch is of various kinds; the lips touch each other in pronouncing pa, pha, etc., the tip of the tongue touches the teeth in pronouncing ta, tha, etc, the tip of the tongue touches the hard palate in pronouncing ṭa, ṭha etc., the middle of the tongue touches the soft palate in pronouncing ca, cha, etc., and the root of the tongue touches the throat in pronouncing ka, kha, etc., In vowels there is no touch. The semi-vowels are produced by slight touch. The sibilants are produced by half touch.

It is not my object here to give the details of the analysis of sound as given in this book. It is distinctly stated that "Dākṣī's son Pāṇini made this analysis known all over the world."

Three more works have to be considered in this connection. These are:—(1) Uṇādi Sūtras, (2) Phiṭ Sūtras and (3) Paribhāṣā Sūtras. The Uṇādi-Sūtras are attributed to Sākaṭāyana by Nāgojī Bhaṭṭa. For it is well-known that Sākaṭāyana held that all words are derivable from verbal roots. Vimala, the author of Rūpamālā attributes is to Vararuci-Kātyāyana. But Goldstücker says that though the Uṇādi Sūtras are not by Pāṇini, yet the list of the Uṇādi suffixes is his.

Phiṭ Sūtras.—Everybody agrees that these sūtras were the work of Sāntanavāchāryya. The sūtras are divided into four sections and number 87 in all. Max Müller would place these sūtras before Pāṇini and assign them to the Eastern School. But Goldstücker on the authority of Indian commentators, thinks that they are posterior to Pāṇini, and that there is no datum to connect them with the Eastern School. One of the Indian commentators says,—" But, on the other hand, these Phiṭ Sūtras when considered with reference to Pāṇini are as if made to-day." And Goldstücker thinks that they were made to criticise Pāṇini. The Phiṭ-sūtras mention the following geographical names :—Sāṅkāśya, Kāmpilya, Nāsikya, Dāru and Ághāṭa. Some of these seem to be more modern than Pāṇini.

There are 134 sūtras in the Paribhāṣā-Pāṭha, at the end of which it is stated that every author of grammar considers shortening his sūtra even by half a mātrā to be as pleasing as the birth of a son. These are axioms or rules of interpretation. Such rules must exist from the beginning of the Sūtra literature. Wherever there are sūtras there must be rules for interpretation of these sūtras. The present Paribhāṣā Pāṭha is a collection made in later times by some unknown author, and their usefulness being apparent, they have been repeatedly commented upon. Even before Pāṇini there existed Paribhāsas. Pāṇini embodied some Paribhāṣās in his sūtras. Kātyāyana added some, and a large number was added by Patañjali. Some of the Paribhāṣās supplement informations given in sūtras,—these are called Jñāpakas; others called Nyāya are applicable to writings other than grammar.

Here ends our brief survey of Pāṇini's Aṣṭādhyāyī, the works attributed to him, and works belonging to his school. I think that this is the proper place to discuss the question of the Vedāṅgas.

The word Vedāṅga and its division into six were known to Kauṭilya and to other, old authors. The theory is that every Sākhā of the Vedas had its six limbs complete. We find that in the matter of Kalpas many Sākhās of the Vedas have preserved their Kalpa works. But of Vyākaraṇa, we get no Vedic treatises. Their place has been entirely taken up by Pāṇini. Pāṇini's predecessor Sākaṭāyana, whose grammer has come down to us, was a Jaina as shown above; and the editor says that he has no rule for *Svara-vaidiki.* So it cannot be regarded as a Vedāṅga. Ápiśali is quoted both by Yāska and Pāṇini, and the only information about his work is that it consisted of eight books. As regards Sikṣā, there are metrical works on this subject, a large number of which is attributed to very very old writers, and they are distributed over many Sākhās of the Vedas. The general opinion is that the Prātisākhyas are Sikṣā works and are very old. But Goldstücker says that they are not Vedāṅgas and are later than Pāṇini, while Max Müller says that the Prātisākhyas are older works and the metrical Sikṣas are later. But Pāṇini's great work, by including the most important principles of Sikṣā in his eight books, has cast both the metrical Sikṣās and the Prātisākhyas into shade. At the present day, these works are very little studied.

Piṅgala, the fourth Sāstrakāra.—After Pāṇini comes Piṅgala. He did for prosody what Pāṇini did for Vyākaṛaṇa. He embodied in his work all the rules of metre and made the Chanda works of different Sākhās go out of currency.

Divyāvadānamālā is a collection of Avadāna stories, made in the 8th or the 9th century A D. But some of the Avadānas in this collection are old. One of these Avadānas is *Pāṅśupradānāvadāna*, which means that in one of his previous births Asoka helped the Buddha of the period by giving him a handful of dust; and the Buddha granted him a boon that in one of his future lives he would be the paramount sovereign of the world. This work is otherwise called Asokāvadāna. It gives the legendary history not only of Asoka but also of the whole of the Maurya Dynasty. Asoka was very naughty in his early youth. So his father Bindusāra thought of sending him to the Āśrama of Piṅgala Nāga. Piṅgala gave him a finished education and predicted his future greatness. The authenticity of the book written many many centuries after Aśoka is very doubtful. This is the only work which calls Aśoka, a Kṣattriya. It is not known where and by whom the Divyāvadānamālā was compiled or the Aśokāvadāna was written. But the tradition embodied in Kāvya-Mīmāṃṣa tempts us to identify the Guru of Aśoka as Piṅgala, the fourth Sāstrakāra who distinguished himself at Pāṭaliputra.

Vyāḍi, the fifth Sāstrakāra—Pāṇini's mother was Dākṣī, the daughter of Dakṣa. Dakṣa's son would be Dākṣi and Dakṣa's descendants more remote than his grandson would be Dākṣāyaṇa. And Vyādi was a Dākṣāyaṇa and a near relation of Pāṇini, possibly the great-grandson or the great great-grandson of his maternal uncle. This Vyāḍi wrote a Saṁgraha extending over 100,000 slokas. But it is not known whether this work was written in prose or in verse, for prose works are often measured by the standard of ślokas of 32 letters each. Patañjali was an admirer of this Saṁgraha. He says,—

शोभना खलु दाक्षायणेन संग्रहस्य कृतिः ।

He says so in connection with the Vārttika II on Pāṇini's Sūtra II, iii, 66, उभय प्राप्तौ कर्मणि which runs—

अकाकारयोः प्रयोगे प्रतिषेधो नेति वक्तव्यं । शेषे विभाषा।

Vyāḍi is quoted several times by Ṛk-Prātiśākhya and Goldstücker says that there is no valid reason for doubting that he was there the same person as the author of the Saṁgraha. I have heard from a Pandit of Benares that Patañjali really commented upon Vyāḍi's Saṁgraha, and his reason was that the first sūtra commented upon by Patañjali is अथ शब्दानुशासनम्. This is not the first sūtra of Pāṇini's Sūtrapāṭha, nor the first sūtra of Katyāna's Vārttika-pātha which is सिद्धे शब्दार्थसम्बन्धे. Vyāḍi is known to later grammarians also. Padmanābha writing his Supadma-Kaumudī in 1394 A.D. in Mithilā frames a sūtra यथा व्यवधानं व्याड़िगालोवयोः Vyāḍi's Saṁgraha is twice quoted by Patañjali in his first Āhnika. From these quotations we can see that unlike Pāṇini he included in his Saṁgraha many topics which are not absolutely necessary in a grammatical work. For instance, he speculates on the eternity and non eternity of the Śabda and so on. We know from Bhartṛhari who writing in the seventh century A. D. says that the Saṁgraha contains 14,000 points and the Saṁgraha is only a part of the Vyākaraṇa Śāstra.

The Sixth Śāstrakāra is Vararuci of the Kātyāyana gotra. He is the author of Vārttikas on Pāṇini's Sūtras. But what is Vārttika? "The characteristic features of a Vārttika," says Nāgojī Bhaṭṭa, "is criticism in regard to that which is omitted or imperfectly expressed in a sūtra." In Nāgojī Bhaṭṭa's words—सूत्रे अनुक्तदुरुक्तचिन्ताकरत्वं वार्त्तिकत्वं।

Their number is 5032. No Vārttikapāṭha of Katyāyana has as yet come down to us. These Vārttikas have been all picked up from Patañjali's Mahābhāṣya. Kaiyata in commenting upon the Mahābhāṣya quotes 34 more Vārttikas. So the number of the Vārttikas known to us is 5066 in all. But in the absence of a manuscript of the Vārttikapāṭha itself it is impossible to say positively which are vārttikas and which are not, and also whether there were other vārttikas or not. These vārttikas are attached to different sūtras of Pāṇini. Kātyāyana takes up a sūtra of Pāṇini and adds vārttikas to it, to supplement the information given in Pāṇini, and also to modify that information according to his own light. In this way he criticises about 1500 sūtras of Pāṇini. The rest go uncriticised.

Now the question is why were so many vārttikas necessary. Pāṇini himself was a very careful man He did everything to the best of his ability. Why was then so much modification necessary ? The reasons are—(i) Pāṇini belonged to the West and Kātyāyana to the East. The Kathā-Sarit-sāgara says that Vararuci-Katyāyana was born at Kauśāmbī which is only 30 miles to the west of the place where the Ganges and the Jumna meet, and is on the southern bank of Jumna. (ii) Several generations intervened between the two. Some of Pāṇini's rules had become obsolete in Kātyāyana's time; new forms of expression had come into vogue.

Goldstücker thinks that the Vājasaneya Prātiśākhya is the work of the same Kātyāyana who wrote the Vārttika on Pāṇini and he is positive that Kātyāyana wrote the Prātiśākhya first and then the vārttika. For he thinks that the object of both these works is the same, viz., to criticise Pāṇini, to think of what is *anukta* and what is *durukta*.

That is perhaps one of the reasons why so many rules of Pāṇini go without criticism in the vārttika. As I have said before, Goldstücker does not think that Prātiśākhyas are included among the Vedāṅgas.

The Kātyāyanas were a powerful family in the East and there were professors of all the Vedas among them. The Sarvānukramaṇī of the Ṛg-Veda is by a Kātyāyana. There is a Kalpasūtra by a Kātyāyana; there is a Gṛhya Sūtra by a Katyāyana, though this has been superseded by Pāraskara-Gṛhya-Sūtra so much so, that in the tradition of the pandits Pāraskara is said to be another name of Kātyāyana. In the Asiatic Society's Library, however, there are manuscripts based on Kātīya Gṛhya Sūtra which is distinct from Pāraskara. There is also a tradition among the pandits that Kātyāyana was the last of the sūtrakāras. They regard his sūtra as the pariśiṣṭa to all the sutras. Besides these, there are 18 pariśiṣṭas to Kātyāyana's Kalpasūtra, all attributed to Kātyāyana himself.. Some other Pariśiṣṭa sūtras are also attributed to him; these are called Kṣepakas, that is, thrown into the Kātyāyana Pariśiṣṭa. All these belong to the Vājasaneya section of the Yajurveda. They are authoritative both to the Mādhyaṃdinas and the Kāṇvas. Chandaga pariśiṣṭa of the Sāmaveda too, is often attributed to Kātyāyana.

If what Goldstücker says is correct, that is, if Vājasaneya Saṃhitā was not known to Pāṇini, the whole family of Kātyāyana except perhaps the writer of Sarvānukramaṇī would come within the period under review in this chapter.

The relation between Kātyāyana and Pāṇini is often misunderstood both in India and in Europe. This misconception in India has given rise to the tradition that Pāṇini and Kātyāyana had a disputation in the court of

Nanda, in which Kātyāyana had always the better of Pāṇini ; but that the mediation of God Śiva made Pāṇini his Sutrakāra and Kātyāyana his Vārttikakāra. European critics say that Kātyāyana was a captious critic, a hostile critic and so on. But the real fact seems to be that Pāṇini collected all the facts of the language existing in his time and evolved sūtras for their explanation. Kātyāyana also did the same. But instead of writing an independent work, he, as a matter of convenience, appended his criticism to Pāṇini's rules. Both are master minds and have laid the whole world under great obligation by collecting all the facts of a progressive language in their time.

Patañjali. The seventh and last Śāstrakāra mentioned in Kāvya-Mīmāṃsā is Patañjali. All that we know about his personal history is that he was the son of Goṇikā and that he belonged to the country of Gonarda which the Vṛhat samhitā places along with Chedi and Kukura in one instance, and with Daśapura and Kerala in another. But he seems to have been very familiar with Ujjaini and Māhiṣmati. Setting from one at sunrise, one could go to the other at sun-set. It is well known that in his time the Greeks under Menander besieged the city of Sāketa and the country of Mādhyamika, which may mean, as suggested, the country round the Udayapura territory. He did not see it himself, but could have seen it if he liked. It is also well-known that he was an officiating priest in one of the great sacrifices held at Pāṭaliputra by Puṣyamitra, the Brahmin general who dethroned the Maurya dynasty early in the 2nd century B. C. and rose to power. He was in Kasmir for some time where he ate rice. His habitual residence appears to have been at some distance from Pātaliputra.

He lived at a time when Aśoka's anti-Brahmanic measures were bearing most disastrous fruits. Aśoka prohibited the slaughter of animals even in sacrifices throughout his vast empire. This was galling to the Brahmins, especially Brahmins professing the Sāma-Veda who were the special priests, so to say, in Somayāga. The Śuṅgas were the Ácharyyas of the Sāmaveda and they are stated in the gotra treatises to be the product of a Niyoga between the Gotras of Bhāradvāja and Viśvāmitra both well-known as fighting Brahmins. So there is no doubt that Śuṅga Puṣyamitra who killed Vṛhadratha, the last Rājā of the Maurya dynasty and assumed supreme power, was a Brahmin and a Sāmavedī Brahmin It is not improbable that on assuming authority he should signalize the event by the performance of a horse-sacrifice by killing hundreds and thousands of animals, not only in the capital city, but perhaps in the very palace of Aśoka, from which the first Rock Edict prohibiting the slaughter of animals was issued. There are some who think that the Brahmins were averse to killing animals because in some of the Upanisads there are such statements as—"मा हिंस्यात् सर्वा भूतानि" "अहिंसा परमो धर्मः" etc., etc. Against one or two such stray expressions of the Upaniṣads, the authority of the Brahmaṇas and the Kalpasūtras, nay the whole Sanskrit literature previous to Puṣyamitra may be cited.

Patañjali's work is called the Mahābhāsya or the Great Commentary, but on which work it is difficult to say. They are not on the sūtras of Pāṇini alone If the vārttikas are attached only to the sūtras of Pāṇini, then the vārttikas given in the first two āhnikas of the first pāda of the first adhyāya of the Mahābhāṣya should not have been included in the Vārttikas of Kātyāyana It may be argued that the second āhnika treats of the Śivasūtras and therefore they may be regarded as a part and parcel of the Sūtrapāṭha of Pāṇini. But that argument does not apply to the first āhnika which treats of the philosophy of Sabda and Artha. In one place (āhnika 1) the question is raised whether Sabda is eternal or produced by a cause. Patañjali says that this has been principally examined in the Saṁgraha and the pros and cons have all been given, and the conclusion has been, that whether it be eternal or produced by a cause, the rules are applicable all the same. In another place too, (āhnika 1) the word Siddha is, on the authority of the Saṁgraha, interpreted as eternal. In another place, while interpreting something like a Vārttika (यथा लौकिकवैदिकेषु) Patañjali makes an uncalled-for remark...प्रियतद्धिताः दाक्षिणात्याः यथा लोके वेदे चेति प्रयोक्तव्ये यथालौकिकवैदिकेष्विति प्रयुंजते। "The people of the south are very fond of Taddhita, therefore instead of saying 'loke' and 'vede' they say, with Taddhita, 'laukika' and 'Vaidika'". Now, who is the Dākṣinātya referred to? He cannot be Pāṇini, a Westerner; cannot be Kātyāyana, an Easterner. May it not be Vyāḍi? May not the whole of the first Áhnika be an exposition of the first portion of the work of Vyāḍi, and the whole of the Mahābhāṣya, an exposition of Pāṇini with Vyāḍi and Kātyāyana; and many of the 5066 Vārttikas be proved to be the dicta of Vyāḍi? There is one such dictum (vārttika 3 on Pāṇini III, iv, 37) in which a vārttika is cited and criticised.

In the first Áhnika there is much which Pāṇini and Kātyāyana would reject as not falling within the province of Vyākaraṇa. The Sivasūtras too, are beyond its province. They properly belong to Sikṣā They are not included in Pāṇini's Sūtrapāṭha. They are there, simply because Pāṇini wanted to use them in that form. In the Aindra School too, which is most ancient and really Srauta, Sarvavarman begins with..."सिद्धो वर्णसमाम्नायः". He took as settled the alphabet as it was then used by the people. Sākaṭāyana did not take the alphabet as actually used by the people, but took it in a Śivasūtra form. His Śivasūtras are thirteen ; and he is more ancient than Pāṇini and writes sūtras for Laukika only, omitting (ऌ) altogether.

In the second āhnika there are many dicta in the form of a vārttika to which Patañjali appends elaborate exegesis. It is suspected that these dicta also belong to Vyāḍi. He was better fitted than Kātyāyana to interpret the Śivasūtra as framed for the benefit of Pāṇini, being a relative. These dicta are couched in a very respectful language

From the third āhnika begin Pāṇini's sūtras and the vārttikas of Kātyāyana mixed up with the dicta, apparently from the saṁgraha of Vyāḍi. For here also we find the same dicta repeated,—यथा लौकिकवैदिकेषु ।

As regards the style of Mahābhāṣya, I may here quote the words of Dr. Kielhorn..."The Mahābhāṣya may be said to be composed in the form of a series of dialogues, and there can be no doubt that its meaning is best brought out by oral discussions among scholars versed in the science of grammar."

The same example, the same principle, and the same explanation are found repeated several times in the book. The principle of a Vaiyākaraṇa attempting to reduce the sūtra in as few syllables as possible, has no place in the Mahābhāṣya. Though it is so, the Mahābhāṣya is far from being diffuse. The author had a large number of authorities before him and his object was to reconcile their views and to give a systematic treatise of Sanskrit grammar, after the fall of the empire of Aśoka, who systematically encouraged the vernaculars. Patañjali had before him not only Pāṇini, Vyāḍi and Yāska and all the authorities quoted by them, but also later authors like Śaunāga and the author of the numerous Kārikās, often quoted in his work. His principal aim was truth, and in finding out truth he did not spare any authority, however ancient and venerable. In one place he says—"Thus Bhāradvāja is completely sent out of court". The theory that Pāṇini wrote sūtras, Kātyāyana made a hostile criticism on them and Patañjali attempted to defend the former is too neat to be true. These were all seekers of truth and all doing their level best to find it out. There were others also, contributing their mite to the solution of linguistic problems Pāṇini rigidly excluded all foreign matter from his sūtras and made his work purely grammatical, that is, etymological. In his time there was the obsolete or obsolescent Vedic speech, the current Sanskrit speech which had some vigorous exponents, notably, Śākaṭāyana, and the vernacular speech mentioned in his Śikṣā as opposed to both the above forms of speech. But vernaculars of Pāṇini's time had very little literature. A change however, came over the spirit of these languages in centuries subsequent to Pāṇini. The great upheaval of the fifth and the sixth centuries produced a large and powerful literature and Patañjali was very anxious to keep the Brahminic tongue free from the contamination of the vernaculars. Perhaps he was requested to undertake the puritanic work by Puṣyamitra himself, with whom he was so closely associated. All the Śāstrakāras received encouragement from the Śiśunāgas, Mauryas and Nandas ; but Patañjali seems to have been specially patronized by the Imperial reviver of Brahminism, Puṣyamitra.

In his time Pāṭaliputra was a great city along the banks of the Śona. Its walls were intact and so were its palaces. There were men to 'teach' Pāṭaliputra, that is, there were guides to Pāṭaliputra. Roads emanated from Pāṭaliputra in various directions : on some of these there were wells here and there. It was more splendid than Sāṅkāśya, but Mathurā was still more splendid than Pāṭaliputra.

As a rule Patañjali did not live in Pāṭaliputra. For he always speaks of going to Pāṭaliputra from this place or that place. Sometimes distances and stages of journey from Pāṭaliputra are mentioned, In a word, he was full of Pāṭaliputra. He speaks of *Chandraguptasabha* and *Puṣyamitrasabha.* In some manuscripts *Chandragupta-sabha* is omitted, but *Puṣyamitrasabha* is always there. He speaks of men going abroad with images of gods and goddesses and making a living from offerings made to them. In one place, he says that when the Mauryas wanted money they used to set up images of gods and goddesses. This is borne out also by Kauṭilya's Arthaśāstra in the Chapter on replenishing treasury in times of war and financial strains. He is more familiar with Gārgyāyaṇas and Vātsāyanas than any other gotra of Brahmins ; and it will be proved in the sequel that the Vātsāyanas had their original home on the Śona in Magadha. Patañjali hints at the revolution which brought about the downfall of the Buddhists and revival of Brahminism in the following words :—आश्चर्य्यं ओदनस्य नाम पाकः। ब्राह्मणानां च प्रादुर्भावः।

"It is a wonder that a meal is called cooking and Brahmins are in the ascendency". Sale of cooked food in the bazar was an institution in Kauṭilya's work, but with the ascendency of the Brahmins every one had to cook his own food. The custom of widow-marriage was looked down upon. But persons marrying widows were not outcasts. There is an oft-repeated statement in Mahābhāṣya— उच्चानि देवदत्तस्य गृहाणि। आमन्त्रयस्वैनं......देवदत्तस्य गावश्चाश्वा हिरण्यं। आढ्यो वैधवेयः।

"Lofty are the houses of Devadatta, invite him...... Cattle, horses and gold Devadatta has (in plenty). He is rich and the issue of a widow". Now, here the word for invitation is *āmantrayasva* and not *nimantrayasva*, for the difference between *āmantraṇa* and *nimantraṇa* is this :

accepting *Nimantraṇa* is obligatory, but in *āmantraṇa* the person invited may come or may not.

The usage of the śiṣṭas is often appealed to in the Mahābhāṣya as a standard of purity. But who is a śiṣṭa ? "In this Aryan settlement (the Áryāvarta), the Brahmins who lay by one year's grain-provision, who are not avaricious, who are disinterested, who are proficient to some extent in any one of the branches of knowledge—these venerable ones are Śiṣṭas." These should study the Aṣṭādhyāyī, the eight books of Pāṇini, but there are some Siṣṭas, who even without studying Aṣṭādhyāyī attain, by intuition or by the grace of God, the correct speech.

The Áryāvarta of Patañjali is not the Áryāvarta of Manu. It is not so extensive as to include the whole country between the Himālayas and the Vindhya. Patañjali's Aryāvarta is limited. It is from the east of Adarśa (which I believe, means the place where the Sarasvati disappears in the desert), to the west of Kālakāvana and from the north of Pāripātra (a chain of mountains joining the Aravalli Hills with the Vindhya) to the south of the Himālayas. All people living outside this area are śūdras. So Sakas and Yavavas, the Sauryas and Kraunchas, the Kiṣkindhyas and Gāndhikas are all śūdras. So are Chandālas and Mṛtapas. So are the carpenters and smiths. So are washermen and weavers. Among these those are regarded as outsiders who contaminate plates by eating, and the contamination is not removed by purification (saṁskāra).

To exhaust all the information which can be gleaned from the Mahābhāṣya is not within the scope of these lectures. In the next lecture you will hear that in Kauṭilya's time there were only three systems of philosophy Sāṁkhya, Yoga and Lokāyata. Kauṭilya does not give any information beyond this. But Patañjali tells us that Bhāguri was the light of Lokāyata. This is perhaps for the first time that we have a really historical name among the writers of the Lokāyata School. Patañjali also speaks of another system of Hindu Philosophy, the Mīmāṃsā ; and Kāsakṛitsni was an eminent Āchāryya of this system with a large following. A Kāsakṛitsna was quoted by Bādarāyaṇa in his Brahmasūtra and Kāsakṛitsni is, according to grammar a son of Kāsakṛitsna. Patañjali quotes also the often quoted verse of the Mahābhārata "Kālah pachati bhūtāni etc." He speaks of Yudhiṣṭhira, Bhīma, Arjuna, Nakula, Sahadeva, Vāsudeva, Satyabhāmā, the Kurus and Ugrasena. He names some poems such as Vāsavadattā, Bhaimaratha, Vararucha-kavya.

The services of Patañjali in Sanskrit grammar are universally acknowledged, but his services as a historian correctly recording contemporary facts are not to be overlooked. The careful study of his book may lead to more important results and correct many of the theories regarding ancient India. One thing may be said here that the tradition embodied in the verse quoted from the Kāvya-Mīmāṃsā completely refutes the theory of Max Müller that Sanskrit went to sleep for seven centuries from the death of Buddha to the rise of the Gupta power in the 4th century A. D. It may be said that this tradition is of as much worth as other Indian traditions, and that so much reliance should not be placed on it. I do not think that Indian traditions are so absolutely worthless ; and when this tradition is borne out by well-authenticated facts, Indians have every right to place absolute reliance upon it.

The encouragement afforded by the powerful dynasties of Magadha, namely the Śiśunāgas, Nandas, Mauryas and Śuṅgas, enabled the Brahmins to perfect a grammatical system of their language in a way which has extorted the admiration of the philologists all over the world. The Brahmins worked upon this theme from generation to generation, from century to century, till Patañjali put the key-stone on their triumphal arch. Every one who has studied Sanskrit grammar knows how patient their researches were, how extensive and yet how accurate. If these dynasties did nothing else but only encouraged these Brahmins, they did not rise into power in vain.

Lecture III.

Chāṇakya's Arthaśāstra.

The discovery of Chāṇakya's Arthaśāstra is a very great event, much greater than the discovery of Yuan Chwang's Travels in Western Countries. Yuan Chwang came to India in 629 A. D. and remained here for sixteen years. Kauṭilya was a native of India, bred up and born here; and he flourished about a thousand years before Yuan Chwang. Yuan Chwang was a mere traveller, at best a devout pilgrim. But Kauṭilya was a politician of pervading genius and he was the Prime-Minister of a great Empire. Yuan Chwang was interested in Buddhism only, and that in its higher phases. But Kauṭilya was interested in everything Indian. Yuan Chwang was a religious man and looked at Indian society from the religious point of view. Kauṭilya was an administrator and a man of the world. His interest in India was that of an administrator and a patriot. Yuan Chwang's account of India was partial and one-sided, that of Kauṭilya thorough and many-sided.

Yet when Yuan Chwang's book was translated and published it revealed a stratum of society which was very little thought of. It was read, studied and almost devoured by all students of Indian History; and it opened a vista of research which was enthusiastically pursued by master-minds of past generations, both in India and Europe. Kauṭilya's Arthaśāstra has not yet aroused that enthusiasm for its study. This is, because its discovery is very recent, not yet twelve years old and its study is not so easy. The Daśakumáracharita justly says "तच्च किल शास्त्रं सर्वशास्त्रानुबन्धि सर्वमेव वाङ्मयं अविदित्वा न तत्त्वतोऽधिगंस्यते" "That Śāstra, they say, is dependent on all Śāstras. Without knowing the whole literature written or oral, it can not be mastered."

That is the reason why it has failed to arouse so far that sort of enthusiasm which Yuan Chwang's charming narrative did. But it deserves close study for years, because it will reveal a picture of ancient India as it was 2300 years ago in every walk of life. Dharma-Śāstras teach us what the society should be—they give the ideal of a society; but this gives the picture of society as it actually was. There are many things in the Artha Śāstra which we do not see anywhere else. There is much that is disgusting, much that is, according to our standard, immoral. But it is a true picture, and a true picture has always a great value, and that value has in this case become enhanced because it is well drawn by a master-hand.

With this preface let us begin to examine the work. It has fifteen books, 150 Chapters and 180 topics; and its extent is 6000 ślokas. The books are:—(i) On the Training of Kings (ii) On Duties of Government Superintendents, (iii) On Civil Laws, (iv) On Criminal Law, (v) On conduct of Administration, (vi) On the Sources of strength of Sovereign States, (vii) On Sixfold Policies, (viii) On Vices and Calamities, (ix) On Invasion, (x) On War, (xi) On Corporation, (xii) On Powerful Enemy, (xiii) On Capture of Forts, (xiv) On Secret Means of Injuring an Enemy, (xv) On Technical Terms. In dealing with these subjects the author displays a wonderful knowledge of the world, of the past history of the country, of the Śāstras studied in his time, of the character and conduct of various races living in the country and around it, of the strategies of war, of the military qualities of the various fighting races and of the minute details of everything connected with the administration of a country. Kauṭilya has a great name even now as an organiser and as an administrator. Every clever man is called a Chāṇakya which is the patronymic of Kauṭilya. He is often compared to Machiavelly and Bismark. Whatever means he might employ, scrupulous and unscrupulous, virtuous or vicious, cruel or benevolent, his sole aim is the peace and prosperity of the Empire; and in his mind the interests of the country and of the king and of the prime minister are identical.

It is a pity that we do not know much about the personal history of such a great master of Politics. Some represent him as a very black and ugly person. But his disciple Kāmandaka describes him as *Sudarśa*, a handsome presence. Indian tradition represents him as very revengeful. He is represented as attempting to destroy the whole species of Kuśa grass, because one of the Kuśa needle pricked him and thus disqualified him for the moment for his ancestral *śrādh*. He is also said to have destroyed the dynasty of the Nandas, because the last of the Nandas insulted him on the occasion of his father's Śrādh ceremony. The present work gives some evidence to the truth of that traditions, when it says that he uprooted the Nandas to avenge himself. The Mudrā Rākṣasa represents him as a poor Brahmin always mindful to the details of Vedic Ceremonies, living in thatched hut, on the roof of which cakes of cow-dung were dried for ceremonial use. As a Brahmin he lived by teaching his pupils taking no advantage of his position as Prime-Minister of a great empire. He was proud of his birth as a Brahmin and addressed his Emperor as Vṛṣala or Śūdra. He is represented as always anxious to retire to private life and employ all the great energy of his mind to the duties of a Brahmin. But his Emperor was grateful to him for his eminent services, appreciated the great qualities of his head and heart and always treated him as his preceptor. Tārānāth tells us that Kauṭilya retired from Premiership on Bindusāra's attaining majority and assuming the reins of Government.

This is in exact consonance with the teachings of our book in Adhyāya 5, Chapter vi, Prakaraṇa xv. In this Prakaraṇa Kauṭilya speaks of the common interest of the king and the Prime-Minister. His teaching in this connection is that when the king is on his death-bed, the Prime-Minister should give out that the king is engaged in some religious ceremony for the prosperity of his kingdom, for the defeat of his enemy, for his longevity or for the birth of a son. He should allow somebody else accompanied with all the paraphernalia of royalty to sit in the court after considerable intervals and make him speak to the courtiers through his own self; or if there is an heir-apparent, he should gradually delegate powers of administration to him and then disclose the news of the king's death. Kauṭilya thinks that the interest of the king and of the Prime-Minister should be absolutely identical.

"No," says Bhāradvāja, an older authority, "when the king is on his death-bed, the Prime-Minister should set up the princes and chiefs against one another and then have them murdered by rousing the subjects against them; or by assassinating them, he should seize the reins of Government. For the sake of Government sons rise against their father and fathers against their sons. Why should the Prime-Minister, the pilot of the kingdom should miss the opportunity which has presented itself to him ? The common saying is. A woman making love of her own accord, curses the man if discarded. Opportunity presents itself once only to one who seeks it. But it never comes again, even when one is ready for action."

"This is," says Kauṭilya, "offensive to body" body politic, unrighteous and unstable. He should install a prince of strong character in the kingdom. In the absence of a prince of strong character, he should bring together the high officials of the state and placing before them a prince of unsteady character or a princess or the queen in the family way he should say, 'This is a trust. Remember his father. Remember your chivalrous character and your high birth. This is a mere flag, (so to say, under which you are to rally). You are the real masters. How should I act ?' To him they reply 'Who else is capable of governing the four castes ? Other than this king under your guidance'. Other ministers should say—'So be it'—and acknowledge the prince or the princess or the queen big with child. He should be shown to cognates and relations and to the ambassadors of the friendly and inimical kings. He should provide the civil and military officers with increased subsistence allowance and salaries, promising that this boy when grown up would do more. And so he should address to the chiefs of forts and outlying possessions, and also to the allies and enemies in a suitable manner. He should take steps to educate the king......... For himself he should not reserve good things. As to the king he should provide him with conveyances, riding animals, jewels, dresses, damsels, palaces and pleasure-gardens. When the king is grown up he should pray for the rest of his mind. If the prince is not pleased with him, he should leave him, otherwise he should continue to follow him. If not liked by the prince, he may retire to a forest or engage himself in a long sacrificial session, after committing his son to the care of men who would undertake to protect his family and wealth. If the king falls under the evil influence of (intriguing) chiefs, he should, as he is an expert in political economy, enlighten the prince by means of history and legends in a way agreeable to him; or assuming the garb of a saint he should try to bring the prince under his influence by showing him miracles, and doing so, should take coersive measures against the seditious."

Kauṭilya's disagreement with Bhāradvāja and the statement of Prime-Minister's duties at a critical time when the king is on his death-bed, shows how deeply loyal he was to the Empire, to the good of which he does not hesitate to sacrifice himself. He asks the Prime-minister to be of unswerving loyalty to the king under all circumstances, even though he is discarded. He asks him to be absolutely selfless in serving the Empire, denying himself all the good things of the world, when he is virtually the master of the empire. Even in his retirement when he is engaged in sacrifices and in Yoga practice, his sole thought is the good of the Empire he has reared up. Such a Prime-Minister is rare and such was Kauṭilya alone. Indian tradition, fragmentary though it is, remembers him in this selfless character.

At the end of the Chapter X of the second book Kautilya says—

सर्वशास्त्राण्यनुक्रम्य प्रयोगमुपलभ्य च ।
कौटिल्येन नरेन्द्रार्थे शासनस्य विधिः कृतः ॥

"Having followed all sciences and having observed practice also, the rules of drawing up writs are framed by Kauṭilya for the benefit of Narendra (Lord of men)."

This ascribes the authorship to Kauṭilya, but it does not name the king for whom it was intended. That piece of information is afforded by the Daśakumárcharita of Daṇḍin in the 8th Chapter in the following words :—

अधीष्व तावत् दण्डनीतिम्। इयमिदानीम् आचार्यविष्णुगुप्तेन मौर्यार्थे षड्भिःश्लोक सहस्रैः संक्षिप्ता।

" Read Daṇḍanīti. This has just now been presented in an abridged form extending to 6000 ślokas by Áchāryya Viṣṇugupta for the benefit of Maurya." This leaves little doubt as to the name of the king. He was Chandragupta Maurya, whose Prime-Minister Kauṭilya was, according to all Indian traditions. The Arthaśāstra says the author was Kauṭilya, while Daśakumāra says, he was Viṣṇugupta. But they were not two different persons. Because at the end, the author himself says :—

दृष्ट्वा विप्रतिपत्तिं बहुधा शास्त्रेषु भाष्यकाराणाम्।
स्वयमेव विष्णुगुप्तश्चकार सूत्रं च भाष्यं च॥

" Having seen discrepancies in many ways on the part of the writers of Bhāṣyas on the Śāstras, Viṣṇugupta has himself written both the Sūtra and the Bhāṣya." If the author describes himself at one place as Kauṭilya and at another place as Viṣṇugupta, Kauṭilya and Viṣṇugupta must be one and the same person. But was the author really the Prime-Minster of Chandragupta in the 4th century B. C.? An answer to this is afforded by another verse at the end of the last chapter :

येन शास्त्रं च शस्त्रं च नन्दराजगता च भूः।
अमर्षेणोद्धृतान्याशु तेन शास्त्रमिदं कृतम्॥

" This Śāstra has been made by him who under provocation quickly rescued from chaos the science of politics and of war, as well as the earth from the hands oef th Naṇdas."

Kāmandaka, an ancient authority on politics is more explicit in giving us an account of the Arthaśāstra and its author. He says :—

यस्याभिचारवज्रेण वज्रज्वलनतेजसः
पपात मूलतः श्रीमान् सुपर्वा नन्दपर्वतः ॥
एकाकी मन्त्रशक्त्या यः शक्त्या शक्तिधरोपमः ।
आजहार नृचन्द्राय चन्द्रगुप्ताय मेदिनीम् ॥
नीतिशास्त्रामृतं धीमानर्थशास्त्रमहोदधेः ।
समुद्दध्रे नमस्तस्मै विष्णुगुप्ताय वेधसे ॥
दर्शनात् तस्य सुदृशो विद्यानां पारदृश्वनः ।
यत्किंचित् उपदेक्ष्यामः राजविद्याविदां मतं ॥

"Salutation to Viṣṇugupta, the veritable Providence, powerful like thunderous fire, by whose thunder-like rites, fell root and branch the mountain-like Nanda Dynasty, firm in all its political strata; who, like Kārttikeya in valour, single-handed, procured by dint of his statesmanship the whole earth for Chandragupta; who, from the ocean-like science of politics churned out, so to say, the nectar of polity. From the observation of that handsome presence who has seen the end of sciences, I shall teach something that has been accepted by the experts of political science."

Kāmandaka speaks of Viṣṇugupta as one, who destroyed the Nanda Dynasty and installed Chandragupta on the throne. The age of Kāmandaka is not known. But he does not seem to be far distant in time from his great master. A perusal of his Nītisāra creates an impression that he was Viṣṇugupta's direct disciple. All the purāṇas which give an account of the dynasties of the Kali Era speak of Chāṇakya as the destroyer of the Nandas and helper of the cause of Chandragupta. Viṣṇupurāṇa; whose account of the dynasties is very short, gives the same account more explicitly.

The personal name of the author is Viṣṇugupta. The name Chāṇakya, he derived from his father's name, Chaṇaka, and the name Kauṭilya, from his gotra. Hemachandra confounds him with Vātsāyana. But Hemachandra is evidently wrong, as one cannot bear two gotra names *i.e.* Vātsāyana and Kauṭilya. He is often confounded with Vātsāyana, the author of the Bhāṣya commentary on the Gautama Sūtra. But this also is untenable. For, Vātsāyana quotes a verse which runs thus :—

प्रदीपः सर्वविद्यानां उपायः सर्वकर्म्मणां ।
आश्रयः सर्वधर्म्माणां विद्योद्देशे प्रकीर्त्तितः ॥

Now, there is a verse in the Arthaśāstra at the end of the first chapter called Vidyāsamuddeśa, or Viddyoddeśa which runs thus :—

प्रदीपः सर्वविद्यानामुपायः सर्वकर्म्मणाम् ।
आश्रयः सर्वधर्म्माणां शश्वदान्वीक्षिकी मता ॥

Evidently it is Vātsāyana who quotes.

Thus far about the author, his book, his king, and his enemy. I proceed now to give a few lessons we can gather from the book :—

(i) The first lesson we learn is that in Chāṇakya's time *i.e.* the latter half of the 4th century B. C. the Atharva-Veda had not yet acquired the same hold on the mind of the Brahmins as the Sāma, Ṛik or the Yajus. It had another associate, the Itihāsa-Veda. The line runs thus :—

सामर्ग्यजुर्वेदास्त्रयस्त्रयी । अथर्ववेदेतिहासवेदौ च वेदाः ।

"The Vedas, Sāma, Ṛik and Yajus, these three constitute

Trayī. There are two more, Atharva-Veda and Itihāsa-Veda. These are the Vedas."

So it seems that in Chāṇakya's time there was a taste for History—and that history is not the History in its narrow sense, of the mere statement of facts and chronology, but history in its widest sense as accepted in modern times. He gives the definition of History in these words :—

पुराणमितिवृत्तमाख्यायिकोदाहरणं धर्म्मशास्त्रं अर्थशास्त्रं चेतीतिहासः ।

"Itihāsa means and includes old tradition, records of events, stories, illustrative anecdotes, religious and civic law and political science", and this history ranked as one of the Vedas, equal in authority with the Atharva-Veda.

(ii) Another lesson we learn is that Sāma-Veda occupies the first position in the Trayī, while Ṛik-Veda has been given that position all through the Vedic period. That is rather curious. Other Vedas, in Sāyana's word, "lived" on the Ṛig-Veda. In the Yajur-Veda there are so many Ṛiks from the Ṛig-Veda and the Sāma-Veda is really the Ṛiks set to music. Then why should Chāṇakya go out of the way and give the first place to Sāma-Veda? Curiously enough. Sri-Kṛishṇa in his Bhagavat-Gītā does the same. He identifies himself with the Sāma-Veda (Vedānām Sāma-Vedosmi). The reason is not far to seek. In the Brāhmaṇa literature and in the Sūtras, Paśu-Yajña and Soma-Yajña are more elaborately treated of than Havir-Yajña which does not derive much assistance from the Sāmans. All the sacrificial rites described in the Pāli Buddhist Literature required immolation of animals, it appears that in the East, originally the country of the Vrātyas, Sāman was held in greater reverence; and Sāma-Vedins were more influential. It is a well-known fact that it was a Sāmavedi Brāmhin, Pushyamitra of the Śuṅga Gotra, who destroyed the Maurya Empire. Probably Chāṇakya was also a Sāmavedi Brāhmin.

(iii) Chāṇakya's Arthaśāstra is based on works of previous writers on the subject; and in the very first chapter, called Vidyāsamuddeśa, he names four schools, which must have taken many centuries to develop. The rudest and the crudest of these Schools is attributed to Uśanas or Śukrāchāryya who is for that reason known as the preceptor of the Asuras, the demons. He teaches that the king's only duty is coertion, condine punishment, assassination and massacre, in other words frightfulness. The next School attributed to Vṛhaspati, the preceptor of the Gods, adds Vārtā to Daṇḍa or coertion. Vārtā is agriculture, commerce and pasture. This is certainly more humane than mere coertion. The next School, attributed to the Mānavas, adds Trayī or the Three Vedas, which had a much more softening influence than Vārtā and Daṇḍa. The last School represented by Chāṇakya adds Ānvikshikī or Philosophy, and includes in it the Atharva-Veda and the Itihāsa too. The development of political ideas from mere coertion to History, Philosophy and the Vedas must have taken centuries. The idea of government in all primitive societies is mere protection of person and property. In the next stage the encouragement of trade, agriculture, commerce and industry is added. Next comes encouragement of education of a religious and social character. Last of all, comes secular education of all sorts. This is the history of the development of political ideas in Europe from the Middle Ages to modern times. Chāṇakya's idea of government appears to be the same as that of the modern age; and it is easy to infer how many centuries elapsed from Uśanas to Kauṭilya.

(iv) The Arthaśāstra says that Ānvikṣikī means and includes Sāṁkhya, Yoga and Lokāyata. From this it is apparent that Nyāya Vaiśeṣika and the two Mīmāṃsās were not then regarded as schools of thought. This is sometimes misunderstood. For the word Ānvikṣikī in modern Sanskrit means only Nyāya-Śāstra, Logic. What the Sāṃkhya and Yoga doctrines were in the fourth century B C., we have no means to ascertain. For, the books extant are much later. The only authentic Sāṃkhya work is the 70 Karikas of Īśvara-Kṛishṇa, composed in the 5th century A. D. or earlier ; and the Yoga-Sūtras are certainly not older. But these *systems* were old. The succession of teachers in the Sāṃkhya School is long, and quotations from many of them have been found in ancient Sanskrit philosophical literature. The Gītā, the Kaṭhopaniṣad and other works contain a system of Sāṃkhya philosophy differing greatly from that of Īśvara Kṛishṇa. So the system took many centuries to develop. That Vaiśeṣika, Nyāya and Uttara-Mīmāṃsā came later has been proved. But the same thing cannot be said about the Pūrva-Mīmāṃsā, which is a direct outcome of the Brāhmṇa and the Sūtra literature of the Vedic schools. But Chāṇakya seems to have omitted it, because it was no part of the Rājavidyā. But the same cannot be true of the Nyāya and the Vaiśeṣika, which every prince should study even in preference to Sāṃkhya and Yoga. Chāṇakya did not mention them because they did not exist at his time. There are certain technical terms of Nyāya and Vaiśeṣika which are not explained in the technical sense by Chāṇakya. They seem not to have assumed that technical sense in his time.

(v) Chāṇakya enjoins to the Sūdras service of the three higher castes, Vārtā (or skilled labour) and profession of actors. So he makes actors Śudras. But they always claim a much higher descent In the last three chapters of Nāṭya Śāstra Kuśīlava or actors are said to have been descended from celestial damsels by human husbands under the following circumstances. Nahuṣa, the king of of the earth conquered for a time the celestial regions and became Indra. There in heaven, Bharata Muni, the founder of the histrionic art entertained him as Indra with some dramatic performance which fascinated him very much. He became anxious to entertain his comrades on earth with the drama, and besought the Muni to descend on earth with the celestial damsels as his actresses. He came with them and lived for a time on earth. But the damsels fell in love with human beings and had children by them. These grew up, relieved their mothers of terrestrial acting and formed a congregation of actors. In a jolly moment some of the actors wrote comedies caricaturing the Ṛṣis.. The Ṛṣis became furious and cursed them to become Śūdras, leading unholy lives. This tradition acquired some support from the statement in the Arthaśāstra.

(vi) Max Müller in his History of Ancient Sanskrit Literature says that the art of writing did not exist in India before the 4th century B. C. Max Müller's theory has not been generally accepted and a controversy is still going on about the antiquity of Indian writing. Now the Arthśāstra says that after the ceremony of tonsure at the age of three, the boy should learn Handwriting and Arithmetic. This evidently shows long use of writing But curiously enough while every first act of the boy, such as his taking of rice for the first time, commencing the Veda, first shaving etc., etc. is celebrated as a sacrament, the first assumption of the pen is not regarded as such. There is no such sacrament in any of the Gṛhya Sūtras of old. The Gṛhya Sutras do not mention it. Yet it was exactly in the same position at Chāṇakya's time as it is now. So writing must have been evolved sometime between the Gṛhya Sūtras and Chāṇakya ; how long before Chāṇakya it is difficult to say. It must have been very early. For there are inscriptions of Buddha's time or even earlier. And Vaśiṣṭha's Dharma-Sūtra which is Pre-Buddhist speaks of *Lekhya* or written documents as the best evidence in a law-suit. But writing was very general in Chāṇakya's time. For King's Edicts used to be written. There was an officer called Lekhaka close by the king. The accountants used to send their accounts in the Audit office in sealed books, the word used being *Pustaka.* In courts of law there were writers, and they used to be fined for not writing what was stated by witnesses or writing what was not stated. So in the 4th century writing was not only generally but very extensively used in all affairs of life ; and boys used to be taught writing from the 4th or 5th year of their life, just as now.

The chapter on writing edicts speaks of penmanship and discourages bad writing. The Sūtra runs thus :—

तत्र कालपत्रकमचारुविषमविरागाक्षरत्वमकान्तिः ।

"Akānti or bad handwriting is writing on black leaves and writing not good to look at, with the letters of unequal size and carelessly drawn." This is just the opposite of what good penmanship should be. That is defined in later literature in these words :—

"समानि समशीर्षाणि घनानि विरलाणि च"

"The letters should be of equal size with their tops in the same straight line and should be closely set together each letter being distinct."

As to the writing materials, they were evidently leaves,

because Kauṭilya uses the word *Patra* i. e. leaf,—leaf of what he does not say. But it is most probable that palm-leaves were used. They were of two kinds, narrow and broad called Tāla and Teḍet. Both these kinds of palms are indigenous in the Malabar Coast and do not grow in Northern India without culture. Palm-trees are to be found in Northern India only in the vicinity of inhabited localities and not elsewhere. It may be that the culture of palm-tree followed the introduction of the art of writing in Northern India.

(vii) At Kauṭilya's time history was extensively cultivated; and, as has been stated before, it was regarded as the Fifth Veda. But very little of that extensive literature has come down to us. The only remnant is to be found in the historical chapters of some of the Purāṇas, viz , Matsya, Vāyu, Brahmāṇḍa, Garuḍa; Viṣṇu aud Bhagavata. But they all referred to one Purāṇa, the Bhaviṣya Purāṇ. Mr. Pergitar has worked up these chapters in his now classical work "Dynasties of the Kaliyuga Era." One peculiarity of these chapters is that while in other dynasties the names only of the kings are given, the dynasties of Magadha contain the duration of the reigns of the kings also. That shows that the art of writing history was a peculiar feature of Magadha. In Kauṭilya's book we get much information about historical facts, which are not known from other sources. When he speaks of the events stated in the Rāmāyaṇa and in the Mahābhārata we are bound to infer that the stories were recorded in some chapter or other of these books. But there are many facts not to be found in them. Here is a list of some of these facts :—Dāṇḍakya, a prince of Bhoja, dishonouring a Brahmin girl through passion, perished with his empire and relations this is found in some recensions of the Rāmāyaṇa. So did Karāla of the Vaideha tribe. Janamejay came to grief by his violence to Brahmins in a fit of anger. So did Tālajaṅgha by his violence to Bhṛigu. Aila perished on account of robbing the four castes through avarice. So did Ajabindu, the Sauvira. Arjuna, a Haihaya prince puffed up with pride disgraced mankind and perished. Intoxicated with prosperity Vātāpi treated Agastya with contumely and was ruined. So were the Vṛṣṇis by their contemptuous treatment of Dvaipāyana" (I, 6, p. 11).

"A brother killed Bhadrasena concealing himself in the room of the queen ; a son killed Kāruṣa, hiding himself in the bed of his mother ; the queen killed Kāśīrāja by fried grain steeped in poison instead of honey ; with anklet smeared with poison the queen killed Vairatnya ; with poisoned gem on her waistband, the queen killed Sauvīra ; with a poisoned looking-glass Jāludha was killed by his queen ; Vidūratha was killed by his queen with weapons concealed in her hair".

These are facts remote both in time and in place, and the fact of stringing them together shows an extensive knowledge of history.

(viii) Sculpture seems to have made when progress when this work was written. For in every fort, at the centre, there used to be temples of the following gods :—Aparājita, Apratihata, Jayanta, Vaijayanta, Śiva, Vaiśravaṇa, the Asvins, Srī and Madirā. Of these Śiva is still worshipped, but more in his phallic emblem than in his image. Vaiśravana after many vissicitudes has become Kuvera. The Asvins were well-known Vedic deities. Srī is Lakṣmī. Others are not at present worshipped. In the corners are installed the Vāstudevatās i. e. the Vasus. Last come the guardian deities of the quarters, these are certainly images. The principal gates were named after Brahmā, Indra, Yama and Senāpati. Most probably there were images of these gods near them.

Just preceding these, containing the names of deities there is a passage which runs thus :—

ततः परम् नगरराजदेवतालोहमणिकारवो ब्राह्मणाश्चोत्तरां दिशं अधिवसेयुः ।

which has been thus rendered by the translator :—"To the North, the royal tutelary deity of the city, ironsmiths, artisans working on precious stones as well as Brahmins shall reside". The translation needs some modification. The word 'devatā' being in the midst of a Samāsa should more fitly be taken with Kāru i. e. artisans, meaning the makers of images of gods for the city and for the royal house. Thus it would imply the existence of image-makers i. e. sculptors.

In another part of the book images of Nāgas have been mentioned. These are certainly not wooden images; because wooden images are separately mentioned in connection with the bed-chamber of the king in the palace, where they are carved on wooden door-frames. If they were not wooden, they must be of stone. But stone images are of two sorts, in bas-relief or in the round. In one case it is expressly stated that it was in the round. Nāga-pratimā, the image of serpents described in page 252 is said to have a hole in it and that hole is not possible in bas-relief.

The deities mentioned are not all of them, Vedic deities. They are mostly Paurāṇika. In the Vadas we do not hear of images. Image-worship is a post-Vedic development; and the less the number of Vedic deities, the greater the distance from Vedic age. Śiva would be the most conspicuous; because he is Īśāna, he is Mahādeva he is Eka-Vrātya and he got Sarvva, Bhava and other five servitors from the quarters as we know from the Vrātya chapter of the Atharva Veda. He is the great deity of the

Vrātyas. We are to infer from this that Śiva-worship in images developed during the interval between the Vedic age and the 4th century B. C. Indra, Brahmā and Vaiśravaṇa were held in great reverence in Buddha's time. Indra was the Lord of the Trayatriṁśa heaven within the Kāmāvacaraloka or the world of desire. Brahmā, Sahāṁpati, had a heaven assigned to him in the world of form, beyond the world of desires; and Vaiśravaṇa is one of the Mahārājās who stand as a connecting link between the earth and heaven. Srī is mentioned in one of the Khilas of the Ṛg-Veda, and she always held a place of moderate reverence through all the ages. Aśvinīkumāras have now disappeared from the Pantheon and is known only as the originator of Medical science of the Hindus. They were the models of beauty, but in that character they are no longer remembered. Senāpati is not known in the vedas. His worship developed after the Śiva legend. Curiously enough, Viṣṇu does not appear at all in the Arthaśāstra. So is Gaṇeśvara

(ix) Kauṭilya did not know Pāṇini. There are many expression in his work which are not approved by Pāṇini. He writes Kriyām for Kuryyām. When using grammatical technical terms he uses the terms of the old grammarians, for instance, when speaking of parts of speech, he uses Nāmākhyātopasarganipātāḥ and not Pāṇini's terms Suvanta and Tiṅanta Pāṇini's book was certainly written before Chāṇakya, but it had not then the currency it acquired a century or two later, when Kātyāyana wrote his Vārttika, Vyādi, his Saṁgraha and Patañjali his Bhāṣya. It is after Patañjali that Pāṇini obtained universal currency.

(x) It has been already stated that there were four schools of polity. But we have 18 different authors quoted in the work besides Āchāryya which Mr. Sham

Sāstry justly considers as his own teacher. He is more often at variance with his own teacher than with others, and that in many of the books. He is at variance with Manu, Vṛhaspati and Uśanas in the book of Vinaya or training of kings and in the book of civil law. He does not quote any other writer on civil law except his Āchāryya. Curiously enough, these very three are the propounders of different schools of Arthaśāstra. The quotations are not from metrical Smṛti but from Sūtra works. They are generally named in the plural.

There is another body of names in the singular on purely political matter. They are Bhāradvāja, Biśālākṣa, Parāśara, Piśuna and Vātabyādhi and Bāhudanti. In several controversies they are quoted in the same order. In one place Ambhīyā is added in the plural at the end. The order seems to be chronological. One seems to improve upon the ideas of the other. For instance, Bhāradvāja says that class-friends should be made ministers. No, says Biśālākṣa they may not obey him. Those who are intimates and know each other's secrets should be appointed. No, says Parāśara, the secrets are mutual. The king also will be in their hands as they in his. Appoint those who are tried in difficulties. No, says Piśuna, this is devotion and not intellect. Appoint those who can show efficient work in administrative matters. No, says Kaunapadanta for they may not have other qualifications of ministers. Appoint descendants of old ministers. No, says Vātabyādhi, they may domineer. Appoint new men. They will be in constant dread of their master. No, says Bāhudanti, they may make blunders. Appoint men of the best family and with highest accomplishments. Kauṭilya says, every one is right. Appoint those men who are fit.

There is another set of names given once only,

Kātyāyana, Kaṇika, Bhāradvāja, Dīrgha-Chārāyana, Ghoṭamukha, Kiñjilka, Piśuna and son of Piśuna. But Kauṭilya does not exhaust the list. These men all speak of the consequences of the displeasure of kings but they speak in enigmatic language. Their statements are only understood by those who know moral stories as given in the Nandi-Sūtra of the Jainas and the Buddhist Jātaka stories Of these, Ghoṭamukha has a *sūtta* in his name in the Dīgha-Nikāya and Dīgha-Kārāyaṇa is mentioned in a Palī Canonical work as my friend Bimalā Charan Law has informed me. They are regarded as politicians and wise men.

Kauṭilya has no mercy for the seditious. They are to be destroyed anyhow ; and as it is hard to punish them openly, they are secretly to be punished by assassination, and for this purpose spies are to be employed in any number. In every department of the state there were spies to watch over the proceedings of the officers—spies with ample power. Spies are to be in every city and everywhere. Kauṭilya's spy-system was wonderful. To the last moment, Rākṣasa in Mudrā-Rākṣasa did not know that his most confidential friend Bhāgurāyaṇa was also a spy of Kauṭilya. He believed in cruel rites prescribed in the Atharva-Veda and has devoted an entire book on these. He uses Mantras other than Vedic These Mantras differ considerably from the modern Tāntric mantras. They have no monosyllabic form such as ' huṁ ' ' phaṭ ' etc. These mantras, the rites and ceremonies conected with them and numerous medicinal substances are put together for the purpose of producing evil consequences on the enemy, in one book, the 14th (and it is called the Upaniṣad.)

But the most interesting part of the work is the 2nd book consisting of 36 chapters. It opens with the colonization of waste lands. Vast tracts of country are to be colonized by establishing villages in it. These are to be protected by forts commanding ten villages, 200 villages, 400 villages and 800 villages. Their approaches are to be guarded by frontier forts. Brahmins are to get lands free. Village-officers get their land free also, but with no power to sell. In each village the old people are to protect the properties of minors and gods. Those who though capable do not maintain their father, mother, sister etc. are to be punished. Any one renouncing the world without providing for the maintenance of their families and dependents should be punished. No ascetic other than Vānaprastha should be allowed to come into the village. Mimicks, dancers, singers, drummers, buffoons and actors should not come to the village. Nor should the village have any building for sports and play. These are some of the village regulations in a new colony. The regulations are very strict. Buddhists, Jainas and other mendicants are strictly prohibited to enter.

Unculturable land should be kept apart for pasture. Larger tracts are to be kept for elephants. Brahmins and Tapasvins are to be given land for sacrificial purposes and penance. At suitable places strong positions surrounded by hills or forests or deserts or trees are to be fortified. Within the fort, a city is to be established, reserving different quarters for different castes, different professions and different classes of labour. Places should be assigned for erecting temples of gods and goddesses. Burning and burial grounds are to be made for different castes; and the distinction is to be strictly observed. Much store is to be laid of all the necessaries and luxuries of life for many years, old stores being replenished by new ones. There should be a treasury, a market-place, godowns for grains and forest produce, an armoury and a jail There should be a mint not only to coin money but also for the purpose of manufacturing ornaments of gold and silver under the control of royal superintendents. Strict regulations were made that the goldsmiths may not cheat their customers. No precious metal was to be purchased at the mine. Widows, crippled women, girls, female mendicants, women working in default of fines, mothers of prostitutes, old maid-servants of the king, temple-girls who have left the temple should be employed to cut wool, fibres, cotton, hemp and silk. They may be made to work on holidays on extra wages. Those women who do not stir out of their houses, those whose husbands have gone abroad, those who are crippled or mere girls, may, when obliged to work for bread, be provided with suitable jobs through the medium of maid-servants. Those women who can present themselves at the weaving-house shall at dawn be enabled to exchange their spinnings for wages. Light just enough to examine the thread shall be kept. If the superintendent looks at the face of such women or talks about any other work, he shall be fined heavily, and more heavily if he delays payment or pays for work not yet done. An establishment like this may be immensely useful in these days of high price of cloths, as suggested by the high prices Committee of Bengal.

The skill of ancient Indian agriculturists is evidenced by the following statement :—" From the Sun, the sprouting of seeds can be told ; from the Jupiter, the bunching of crops, from Venus the rainfall is foretold."

About liquor-shops. "Liquor-shops should contain many rooms, provided with beds and seats. The bed-room should contain flower, water and other things as suit the season. Spies stationed at the shops shall ascertain whether the expenditure incurred by the any customers in the shop is ordinary or extraordinary and also whether there are any strangers. They shall also ascertain the value of the dress, ornaments and gold of the customer, lying there insensible under the influence of wine. If they lose anything, the shop-keeper shall have to make it good and pay an additional fine. Merchants seated in half-closed rooms should observe the appearance of local and foreign customers who in real or false guise of Āryas sleep there with their mistresses.

Slaughter-House :—Cattle such as calf, bull or milch-cow shall not be slaughtered. He who slaughters or tortures them to death shall be fined 50 *paṇas*.

Municipal Regulations :—Managers of Charitable Institutions shall send information to the Sthānika or Gopa as to any heretics or Pāṣaṇḍas and travellers arriving to reside therein.

Whoever throws dirt in the street shall be punished with ⅛th of a *paṇa*. Whoever causes mire or water to collect in the street shall be fined ¼th of a *paṇa*. Whoever commits the above offences on the king's road shall be punished with double the above fines. Whoever commits nuisance in places of pilgrimage, reservoirs of water, temples and royal buildings shall be punished with fines from one paṇa upwards in accordance with the gravity of the offences. But when they do so on account of the use of any medicine or on account of any disease or from fright, no fine shall be imposed. Whoever throws inside the city the carcasses of animals such as cats, dogs, mongooses and snakes shall be punished with a fine of 8 paṇas ; of animals such as ass, camel, mule and cattle, 6 paṇas. Whoever throws corpses shall be punished with a fine of 50 paṇas.

The Buddhists and Ājīvakas are mentioned by name only once in p. 199, " He who entertains in worship or

Śrāddha, Śūdra mendicants such as a Buddhist or an Ajīvaka shall pay a fine of 100 paṇas." Kauṭilya is very hard upon Pāṣaṇḍīs or professors of other religions.

He says in p. 242 that active spies should consider the property of congregations of priests as a trust in the hands of a dead man; and the property of gods not enjoyable by the Śrottriyas as belonging to one whose house has been burnt (and is homeless).

Lecture IV.

The Vātsyāyanas were settled in Magadha from very remote antiquity. They were descendants of Cyavana and lived in the holiest of holy places in Magadha, namely, the hermitage of Cyavana situated five miles to the east of the Śoṇa. Cyavana was the son of Bhṛgu, son of Brahmā by Paulomī, the daughter of Pulomā Rākṣasa. Cyavana married the daughter of Śaryāta and had a son by her, named Dādhīca. Dādhīca was bred up and born at the capital of Śaryāta who was so fond of him that he never allowed him to go to his father at the hermitage. He received a finished education at the capital and was regarded as the most accomplished young Ṛṣi of his time. The king then allowed him to go and see his father. With a suitable escort, he reached the west bank of Śoṇa, otherwise called Hiraṇyavāha. He heard of two celestial damsels practising austerities close by, and thought it his duty to pay homage to them. The younger girl fell in love with him at first sight and the young Ṛṣi loved her in return. The celestial damsels were no other than Sarasvatī and Sāvitrī. The first was cursed to live on the earth by Durvāsā at the court of Brahmā and the second accompanied her out of affection. The hermitage was only five miles from the place where Sarasvatī lived and the lovers had their own way. The consequence was that a son was born to them. Sarasvatī gave him all the knowledge she possessed. But as the curse ended with the birth of a son, she had to return to heaven, entrusting her son to the care of Akṣamālikā, the wife of her husband's brother. Dādhīca renounced the world and the son, too, followed suit, when he came of age. But before he did so, he imparted all his knowledge, received from his mother, to his cousin Vatsa. And from Vatsa proceeded the eminent family of the Vātsyāyanas noted for their learning. They settled at Prītikūṭa within the boundaries of the hermitage.

Bāṇabhaṭṭa, a Vātsyāyana gives this account of the origin of his *Gotra* and family in the first chapter of his *Harṣacarita* in the beginning of the 7th Century A.D. That the account is very ancient is proved by two circumstances :—(1) The advent of two celestial beings in their celestial forms to earth and leaving a progeny behind is of a piece with the story of Pururavas and Urvaśī, the story of Śakuntalā, and the story of celestial nymphs coming down to earth under Nahuṣa. In more modern times they do not come in their celestial forms, but are born as human beings and live till the termination of the curse. (2) It records the origin of a *gotra*. As yet, no account of the local origin of a Gotra has been found anywhere. The account of the local origin of the Vātsyāyana Gotra is, therefore, a piece of information of the highest value. That the Vātsyāyanas were settled at the hermitage of Cyavana from a very remote antiquity is proved by the fact that Patañjali is full of Vātsyāyanas, as he is full of Pāṭaliputra, living as he did, very near the great city of old, when engaged in writing the Mahābhāṣya.

It may appear curious that Magadha which was regarded with so much aversion by the Vedic Aryans should be the home and settlement of Ṛṣis such as Cyavana, Dāḍhīca and Vatsa. The reason is not far to seek. These most probably belonged to the converted Vrātyas, who had a special attraction for Magadha at the later stage of the Vedic era.

It may be urged that there were two Gotras under the name of Vātsyāyana, one mentioned in Baudhāyana's *Mahāpravarādhyāya* as descendants of Bhṛgu. Cyavana, Āpnavat, Aurva and Jāmadagnya ; and the other mentioned in Matsya Purāṇa as descendants of Kaśyapa. But in his chart of Gotrapravara, Mr. P. Chentsal Rao, C.I E., says that many descendants of other Ṛṣis were affiliated to the family of Bhṛgu and so the Vātsyāyanas, descended from Bhṛgu and those descendants from Kaśyapa may be one and the same family.

In the Matsya Purāṇa again, the Vātsyāyanas were closely allied to Kauṣītaka who were undoubtedly Vrātyas, as we know from Tāṇḍya Mahābrāhmaṇa. This is further borne out by the fact that "Mahāpravarādhyāya" puts the Vatsyāyanas in the list of Gotras who are regarded as *Kevala-Bhṛgus*, that is, not attached to any of the eight *Gotra-pravartakas* : Jamadagni, Bhāradvāja, Viśvāmitra, Atri, Gotama, Kaśyapa, Vaśiṣṭha, and Agastya. Of these Jamadagni is a descendant of Bhṛgu. The other descendants are known as *Kevala-Bhṛgus*. They differ from other Brāhmaṇas in that they can marry in any Gotra except those, the majority of whose Pravaras agrees with theirs ; while other Brāhmaṇas cannot intermarry, if they have a single Pravara Ṛṣi in common. My contention, therefore, is that these Kevalas came to the fold of the Vedic Aryans at the latter end of the Vedic Period from among the Vrātya Aryans, about whom I have said so much in my first lecture.

The earliest work of the Vātsyāyanas is perhaps the

Kāmasūtra. The commentator says that the author's personal name was Mallanāga and that his Gotra name was Vātsyāyana. The work follows in the footsteps of Kauṭilya, the author of Arthaśāstra. It has seven Adhikaraṇas or books, 36 chapters, and 64 Prakaraṇas or topics. Its extent in ślokas is a thousand and a quarter. But unlike Kauṭilya, it gives the tradition of the Śāstra first, and then gives its contents. Kauṭilya does not give the tradition at all. They are to be inferred from his quotations.

The tradition of the Kāmasūtra is exceedingly interesting. It says that Prajāpati after the creation, delivered a work in one hundred thousand chapters on the three aims of human life. These three aims are :—Dharma, Artha and Kāma (Law, Economics and Erotics) Manu "separated" the portion assigned to Law; and Vṛhaspati that to Economics; Nandi the follower of Mahādeva "separated" Erotics in one thousand chapters. Auddālaki Śvetaketu abridged Erotics in five hundred chapters. Pāñcāla Bābhravya abridged Śvetaketu's work in one hundred and fifty chapters divided into seven Adhikaraṇas or books, namely, :– (i) Sādhāraṇa (preliminary), (ii) Sāmprayogika (union), (iii) Kanyāsamprayuktaka (inducing of girls), (iv) Bhāryyādhikaraṇika (section about a wife) (v) Pāradārika (adultery) (vi) Vaiśika (about public women) (vii) Aupaniṣadika (secrets).

Later on, at the request of the public-women of Pāṭaliputra, Dattaka wrote an independent and exhaustive treatise on the 6th subject, that is, on public-women, namely Vaiśika. The commentator notes the following tradition about the author Dattaka. A Brahmin from Mathurā migrated to Pāṭaliputra. A son was born to him at his old age. The mother died at child bed, and the father gave the child to a Brāhmaṇī, who named him

Dattaka (because he was given to her). The boy grew up, acquired a knowledge of all the Śāstras and all the fine arts. On account of his great skill in the exposition of the Śāstras, he became famous as Dattakācāryya. Attaining maturity, he was anxious to learn the ways of the world, which, he thought, could be best learnt from public-women. So he went to their quarters every day and learned their ways; so thoroughly did he learn, that at last they used to come to him for advice in matters erotic. Then Vīrasenā and other noted courtesans of Pāṭaliputra requested him to write a treatise on the art of winning lovers.

The example of Dattaka proved catching. Learned men were not wanting to try their skill in the other six subjects of erotics. So Cārāyaṇa wrote a treatise on the preliminaries, Suvarṇanābha on union, Ghoṭakamukha on girls, Gonardīya on wives, Gonikāputra on adultery and Kucumāra on the secrets of the science. Thus many authors wrote independent treatises on some topics or others of erotics. They were difficult to collect and difficult to study, while Bābhravya's work was too extensive to be mastered. So Vātsyāyana abridged Bābhravya's work. Thus the present work came into existence.

Patañjali, the author of the Mahābhāṣya was the son of Gonikā and was born in Gonarda. But he cannot be identified with the authors of Bhāryyādhikaraṇika and Pāradārika sections, because they are apparently two different persons. Ghoṭakamukha is quoted not only in Kāmasūtra but in Arthaśāstra too. They do not seem to be one and the same person Because Ghoṭamukha is not a personal name but the name of a Gotra. So it is with Cārāyaṇa, a Gotra name.

Attempts have been made to prove that Cārāyaṇa and Ghoṭakamukba in the Arthaśāstra of Kauṭilya, in the

Kāmasūtra of Vātsyāyana and in the Pāli Literature are identical. But that seems to be impossible For the father of Dattaka came from Mathurā to Pāṭaliputra. He or his son Dattaka would be a contemporary of Kauṭilya. For, Pāṭaliputra was made capital in the 4th year of Udayī ; and the Brāhmaṇa who came there seem to have been attracted by the fact that it was the capital of a big monarchy. Supposing that the removal of capital from Rājagṛha had taken place in 440 B. C and Kauṭilya had been there in 325 B.C., the Brāhmaṇa or his son Dattaka would be contemporaries to Kauṭilya who was then advanced in years. Dīgha-Cārāyaṇa and Ghoṭamukha wrote on erotics after Dattaka. So Kauṭilya could not have quoted from them. So Cārāyaṇa and Ghoṭamukha, whom Kauṭilya quotes cannot be the same who are quoted by Vātsyāyana. Those quoted by Kauṭilya were story-tellers. Those in the Pāli Literature were religious men and politicians. And those quoted by Vātsyāyana were authors of erotics. To identify these would be rather audacious. A Suvarṇanābha has been mentioned by Rājaśekhara in his *Kāvya-Mīmāṃsā* as an author of poetics. It would be very bold to attempt to identify him with our Suvarṇanābha, because Poetics is a much younger science.

Śvetaketu is a well-known figure in Vedic Literature He was a contemporary of Pravahana Jaivala and also of Janaka of Videha. He belonged to the latter end of the Vedic period. But he is better known as the Ṛṣi who instituted marriage and who is likely to have written an extensive work on erotics. Some of his ideas are very primitive and crude. But he seems to be a historical person and there is nothing to prevent our thinking that he was the original propounder of the science, as he was the founder of the marriage system.

The next author is Pāñcāla Bābhravya. His book was studied by Vātsyāyana. For Vātsyāyana distinctly says,—

Bābhrabyīyāṃśca sūtrārthān āgamayya vimṛśya ca.
Vātsyāyanaścakāredaṃ Kāmasūtraṃ yathāvidhi.

So Vātsyāyana studied Bābhravya's work with his Guru. Mr. Jayaswal thinks that the book may yet be found by a careful search, for it is quoted in such a late work as Pañcasāyaka The arrangement of the 500 chapters in Auddālaki's work is not known It was not divided into seven Adhikaraṇas. For, the credit of making that division is given by Vātsyāyana to Bābhravya Pāñcāla Most likely Auddālaki wrote more on union or Samprayoga than on other subjects He divided that subject into ten major heads. So his work was called Daśatayī. At the first introduction of marriage system it is just in the fitness of things that he should abstain from dwelling upon the duties of a chaste wife, of a girl wife and of a public-women, nay upon adultery, there being no marriage at or before his time. It is in fact in a society which regards marriage as an ancient and sacred institution, that Bābhravya's book in seven Adhikaraṇas is possible. Bābhravya divided the ten major heads of union into sixty-four parts or Kalās. He did not sub-divide each division into eight, but the sum-total of the sub-divisions was sixty four.

Ṛgveda was originally divided into ten Maṇḍalas. Therefore it used to be called Daśatayī But in the Pāñcāla country it was divided into Aṣṭakas and each Aṣṭaka into eight Adhyāyas and it is therefore called Catuḥṣaṣṭi. The entire Kāmaśāstra, too, consisting of union only, was originally divided into ten parts and Bābhravya Pāñcāla reduced it into sixty-four Prakaraṇas or topics. He also reduced the subject of union dealt with in the second Adhikaraṇa into eight sections and about sixty-four sub-sections Therefore the Bāhvṛcas or Ṛgvedī Brahmins used playfully and wickedly to call Kāmaśāstra "sixty-four." The term sixty-four applied to Kāmaśāstra, says Vātsyāyana, is appropriate; because like the Ṛgveda it has its ten parts as well as sixty-four. And the author of the change in both cases was a Pāñcāla. "Pāñcāla-sambandhācca."

Improving upon this the commentator says, "Pāñcālena Maharṣiṇā Ṛg-Vede catuhsaṣṭir-nigaditā Bābhravyenāpi Pāñcālena svakṛte Sāmprayogike adhikaraṇe āliṅganādaya uktāḥ: tataśca dvayorekagotranimittasamākhyena Pāñcālena nigadanāt sambandho'steva"

The word Pāñcāla does not seem to denote a country but a Gotra. And there is a Pāñcāla Gotra among the descendants of Kaśyapa. The Gotra might have derived its name from the country of Pāñcāla, its original home But there is no certain indication that the works were re arranged in the Pāñcāla country. The information, that a Ṛṣi of the Pāñcāla Gotra re-arranged the Ṛgveda, is however, of the highest importance, in as much as, this Gotra belonged to the later Vedic Period and that it had something to do with the Pāñcāla country. Nothing up to this time was positively known about the author of the re-arrangement of the Ṛgveda from Maṇḍala to Aṣṭaka. That Pāñcāla is not a country but a Gotra is clearly stated in the commentary quoted above. So Bābhravya here, is a mere patronymic and not a Gotra, though a Bābhravya Gotra is enumerated amongst the descendants of Viśvāmitra.

Classifications of the Śāstras.

Kauṭilya classifies all sciences under four heads, Ānvīkṣikī, Trayī, Vārtā and Daṇḍanīti, that is, Philosophy, Religion, Economics and Politics. But he is concerned only with the Rājavidyā or Royal Studies; they are not in fact a classification of all the sciences known in his time. Vātsyāyana is more explicit and comprehensive. He classifies all human studies under Trivarga,—Dharma, Artha and Kāma. Mokṣa he mentions in one of his Sūtras, but after that he drops it altogether. He says that Dharma is to be learned either from Śruti (which includes Smṛiti) or from the learned. Artha or Economics is to be learned from the conduct of Royal officers or from experts. Kāma he defines generally as the enjoyment of the objects of all the senses but then restricts to its ordinary sense. It is to be learnt from the Kāmasūtra and from Nāgarakas. Artha, says Vātsyāyana, is more important than Kāma and Dharma is more important than Artha.

Comparing classifications of the Śāstras by Kauṭilya and Vātsyāyana it appears that Dharma is a more comprehensive term than Trayī and includes Ānvīkṣikī too. Artha is more comprehensive than Vārtā. Kāmaśāstra is not at all included by Kauṭilya either in its general or in restricted sense. So Vātsyāyana represents a more advanced thought than Kauṭilya.

There were men in Vātsyāyana's time who did not believe in the utility of these studies which they strenuously opposed. Vātsyāyana is at great pains in meeting their arguments. In the matter of the study of Dharma, his principal opponents were the Lokāyatikas. Kauṭilya's Arthaśāstra mentions them as a school of philosophy. Patañjali says that one of their principal writers was Bhāguri. But Vātsyāyana quotes a Sūtra from their Philosophy—

(1) Varaṃ sāṃśayikāt niṣkāt asāṃcāyikaḥ kārṣāpaṇaḥ.

This is the first undoubted quotation that has been found from their original Sūtras. But I think that the whole section of the Kāmaśāstra opposing the utility of the study of Dharma consisting of five Sūtras is directed against the Sūtras of Lokāyātika. These are :—

(1) Na dharmāṃścaret—Eṣyatphalatvāt sāṃśayikatvāt ca. (2) Kobyavāliso hastagatam paragataṃ kuryyāt. (3) Varamadya kapotaḥ śvo mayūrāt.

It may be said in this connection that at the present moment the knowledge of the doctrine of the Cārvāka or the Lokāyatika School is confined to two quotations. One in the seventeenth canto of Naiṣadha-Caritaṃ and the other in the first chapter of *Sarvadarśanasaṃgraha*. Both are in verse and not in prose or Sūtra form. The name of the Sūtrakāra is given in one place as Vṛhaspati :—

Agnihotraṃ trayo vedāḥ tridaṇḍaṃ bhasmapuṇḍrakaṃ
Prajñāpauruṣahīnānām jiviketi Vṛhaspatiḥ.

In one place the fourth pāda reads "*Jivikā Dhātṛnirmitā.*"

Another account of their Sūtra has been found in the *Saḍdarśana-Samuccaya* of Haribhadra who died in Samvat 585. Here the author devotes several Kārikās to illustrate the Lokāyatika doctrines. The commentator Guṇaratna quotes a verse from Vācaspati which is only another name of Vṛahaspati :—

Pṛthivyaptejovāyuriti tattvāni tat samudāye. Śarīrendriyasaṃjñā tebhyaścaitanyaṃ.

(Page 307 of Saḍdarśana Samuccaya. Bibl. Ind. Ed.). This agrees completely with the opinion of Ajitakeśakambala as quoted by Mr. Ui in his Introduction to the Vaiśeṣika Philosophy, p. 19-20. I give the whole passages in full. "Ajitakeśakambala contends that a human body is built up of the four elements (Caturmahābhūtika); when he dies, the earth in him relapses to the earth and the fluids to the water, the heat to the fire, the winds to the air and his faculties (Indriyāni, the five senses and the mind as the sixth) pass into space (Ākāśa). On this

Mr. UI remarks,—"The opinion is real and radical Materialism. There is no soul, nor any other mental factor but only the five sorts of materials. Body is the combination of five elements and the soul is nothing but the body. Ajitakeśakambala is probably a Cārvāka."

Kauṭilya in his Arthaśāstra says that Vṛahaspati and his followers said that Royal Studies should be confined to Economics and Politics, excluding Philosophy and Vedas altogether. There is an Indian tradition that Vṛahaspati was a Nāstika, and I have often been asked to search for a Vṛahaspati Sūtra of the Cārvāka School. May not the Sūtras as quoted here from part of Vṛahaspati's work ?

Vātsyāyana quotes two more Schools closely related to the Lokāyatikas. They are called Kālakāraṇikas and the other Arthacintakas. The commentator speaks of another school, Īśvarakāraṇika. Three Sūtras are quoted as from the Arthacintaka School. They are—

Bahavāśca Kāmavaśagāḥ sagaṇā eva vinaṣṭāḥ śrūyante. Tathā Dāṇḍakyo nāma Bhojaḥ kāmāt Brāhmaṇa-kanyām abhimanyamānaḥ sabandhurāṣṭro vinanāśa. Devarājaścāhalyāmativalaś-ca Kīcako Draupadīm Rāvaṇaś-ca Sītām apare cānye ca vahavo dṛśyante kāmavaśagā vinaṣṭā ityarthacintakāḥ.

Of these three the second is to be found *ad verbatim* and *ād literatim* in the Arthaśāstra of Kauṭilya. The two other Sūtras may also have come from the Arthacintakas. Kauṭilya has many more examples, because he had to show evil consequences of all the six different passions ; while the present author has to show the consequences of lust alone.

The time of Vātsyāyana. The time of Vātsyāyana can be determined by the ages of authors whom he quotes and authors who quote him or by the age of events recorded in his book. He quotes from

Auddālaki, Bābhravya-Pāñcāla, Dattaka, Cārāyaṇa, Ghoṭamukha, Suvarṇanābha, Kucumāra, Gonardīya Gonikaputtra. But the exact date of none of these authors is known So these afford us no clue to his date. The only thing that is known for certain is that Dattaka belonged to Pāṭaliputra. The upper limit of his age is that he might be a contemporary of Kauṭilya. But the lower limit of his age is not known. Vātsyāyana mentions one event, a pathetic scandal in the palace of Kuntala Sātakarṇī Sātavāhana. He was the 13th king of the Andhra dynasty and may be placed in the 1st century B.C. And Vātsyāyana flourished at a time when the memory of the scandal was fresh So he may be placed in the first century A.D. ; for, the public memory is very short and in one or two generations, people forget these scandals. There are other events also recorded in the Kāmasūtra. Naradeva whom the commentator speaks of as a General of the Pāṇḍya kings, killed a dancing girl and Colarāja killed a public-woman, Citrasenā by name. But the names of the kings of Pāṇḍya and Cola are not mentioned and we are at sea as to their chronology. Vātsyāyana mentions Ābhīra Koṭṭarāja who was killed by a washerman employed by his brother when the Rājā entered another man's house to find out his lady-love. The commentator has enlightened us only so far as that Koṭṭa was the name of a place in Gujarāṭa. But we know nothing of Koṭṭa, and Gujarāṭa is a very later name, not so old as Vātsyāyana. The country was so named after the advent of the Gurjaras. The commentator also tells us that Ābhīra is the name of a Rājā and not of a tribe. Vātsyāyana also says that Jayatsena, king of Kāsī was killed by the commander of his horses. That also does not help us in finding any clue to the date of our author. I am not in a position from the meagre facts known up to date of Indian History, to hazard a conjectural date of Vātsyāyana. All that I can assert is that he seems to have come two or three generations after Kuntala Śātakarṇī.

There is another way of determining the time of Vātsyāyana. Take all the countries mentioned by him and see in what century they existed as social units. For with political units our author had absolutely nothing to do. To him Kuntala Śātakarṇī, Naradeva, the Pāṇḍya General, the Cola Rājā were all on the same level. The tribes and tribal countries mentioned by him are Andhras, Vatsagulmakas, Vaidarbhas, Aparāntakas, Saurāṣṭrikas, Ābhīrakas, Strairājyakas, Gauḍas, Saindhavas, Haimavatas, Prācyas, Vaṅgas, Aṅgas, Kaliṅgas, Nāgarakas, Madhyadeśakas Vālhīkas, Avantikas, Mālavas, Ābhīras, the land enclosed by six rivers (with the Sindhu as the sixth), Lāṭa, Kośala, Sāketa, Ahicchatra, Saurasena Mahārāṣṭra, Draviḍa, Vānavāsika and Cola. The commentator gives some accurate directions for finding out these countries or the habitations of these tribes. For instance he says—

Prācyā Aṅgāt pūrveṇa (Bombay Edition p. 171). Sāketā Ayodhyakāḥ (p. 172 *ibid*). Nagarakāḥ Pāṭaliputrakāḥ (p. 172). Śaurasenāḥ Kauśāmbyāḥ, Kālindyāḥ dakṣiṇataḥ kule ye nivasanti (p. 172 *ibid*). Strīrājyās-Tripurī tatra bhavānām (p. 322 *ibid*). Gauḍāḥ Kāmarūpakāḥ Prācyaviśeṣāḥ (p. 302 *ibid*). Saindhavānām Sindhunāmā nadastasya paścimena Sindhudeṣas-tatra bhavānāṃ (p. 302 *ibid*). Haimavatānāṃ Himavad-dronī-bhavānaṁ (p. 302 *ibid*). Aṅgāḥ Romarāhityāt (?) pūrveṇa Aṅgāḥ (p 302 *ibid*). Kaliṅgāḥ Mahānandyāḥ pūrveṇa Kaliṅgāḥ (p. 302 *ibid*). Vaṅgāḥ Gauḍaviṣayād dakṣiṇena Vaṅgāḥ (p. 302 *ibid*).

The passage giving a description of Aṅga, Vaṅga and Kaliṅga is hopelessly corrupt. The Benares Edition reads—

Vaṅgāḥ Lauhityāt pūrveṇa, Aṅgāḥ Mahānadyāḥ

pūrveṇa, Kaliṅgāḥ Gauḍaviṣayāddakṣiṇena (p. 295 Benares Edition).

I do do think the Benares Edition improves matters much.

Vatsagulmakāḥ Dakṣiṇāpathe sadaryyau Rajputrau Vatsagulmau tābhyāmadhyavasito deśo Vatsagulmaka iti pratītaḥ (p. 295, Bombay Edition). Vaidarbhāḥ Kālañjarāddakṣiṇena Vidarbho nāma deśas-tatra bhavānāṃ (p. 288, Benares Edition). Paścimasamudra-samīpe Aparāntadeśaḥ (p. 130, Bombay Edition). Lāṭaḥ Apara-Mālavātpaścimena Lāṭaviṣayaḥ (p. 130 *ibid*). Vajravantadeśāt paścimena Strīrājyaṃ (p. 130 *ibid*). Benares Edition reads Vaṅgarakta in the place of *Vajravanta* (p. 126, Benares Edition). Andhra iti Narmadāyā dakṣiṇena deśo Dakṣiṇāpathaḥ tatra Karṇāṭa-viṣayāt pūrveṇa Andhra viṣayaḥ (p. 130, Bombay Edition). Mahārāṣṭrakā iti Narmadā Karṇāṭaviṣayayor-madhye Mahārāṣṭraviṣayaḥ (p. 131, *ibid*). Nāgarikā iti Pāṭaliputrakāḥ (p 131 *ibid*). Draviḍa iti Karṇāṭa-viṣayāddakṣiṇena Draviḍaviṣayaḥ (p 131 *ibid*). Vanavāsaḥ Kuṅkanaviṣayāt pūrveṇa Vanavāsaviṣayaḥ (p. 131 *ibid*). Ābhīradeśaḥ Śrīkaṇṭha-Kurukṣetrādibhūmiḥ (p. 130 *ibid*). Mālavyā iti pūrva-Mālavabhavāḥ. Ávantikāḥ Ujjayinīdeśabhavāḥ tā eva Apara-Mālavyāḥ.

Most of these countries are known in ancient works like the Brāhmaṇas, the Sūtras, Kauṭily's Arthaśāstra, the Mahābhārata, and in Aśoka's inscriptions. Vanavāsī seems to be rather modern. The ancient name of the district Śimogā in Mysore was Jayantī or Vaijayantī It became known as Vanavāsi about a century or two before the Trinetras rose to power. The Trinetras were superseded after four or five generations by the Kadambas, who became Kṣatriyas from Brāhmaṇas, and who seem to have come to power in the early third century A. D.

The fifth king of this dynasty, Kākutsthavarmā declares that he was a friend of the Guptas in the south. Lewis Rice in his work entitled, "Mysore and Coorg from Inscriptions" thinks that the Gupta king mentioned by Kākutsthavarmā is no other than Samudragupta who in his Digvijaya came to the south in the middle of the fourth century A. D. (See Rice, Chap. on the Kadambas). Vaijayantī, therefore, became Vanavāsī about the begining of the Christian Era.

The country named Saurāṣṭra is known to Kauṭilya. The whole of Saurāṣṭra or a part of it to the west of Apara-Mālava was known to Ptolemy in the middle of the second century A. D. as Laria. The country seems to have acquired that name, a century or so earlier than Ptolemy. Laria in Sanskrit would be Lāṭa, and Lāṭa is known to Vātsyāyana. Therefore, Vātsyāyana can be easily placed in the first century A. D.

The Epigraphical remains in Ahicchatra range from the second century B. C. to the third century A. D. So in the first century A. D. Ahicchatra was a well-known place and Vātsyāyana says that the people of Ahicchatra were rather puritanic in their dealings with public women. From these considerations, I place Vātsyāyana in the first century A. D. As I have said before, the knowledge of Indian Chronology has not advanced much so as to enable students to fix the date and year of the composition of any great Sanskrit work of old. It is enough, if we are approximately within a century in this matter.

The above, however, is a dry and rather unengaging account of historical facts that may be gleaned from the Kāmaśāstra. But there is another aspect of the work which is much more engaging and much more attractive, I mean the pictures of the society at the time—pictures of a living society as seen and experienced by the author round about him. I will now attempt to present to you some of these pictures. In the very first book, Vātsyāyana gives the picture of a Nāgaraka. I am at a loss how to translate the word in English. Literally it means the "Citizen" But "Citizen" will not convey all the meanings of Nāgaraka. The word "Dandy" has a bad odour about it. "Gallant does not express the social aspects of Nāgaraka. I, therefore, in my poverty of English, should like to translate it as a "fashionable man." His first qualification is that he should be well read. His second qualification is that he should be a married man. His third qualification is that he should have competence, either by inheriting a fortune from his ancestors, or by acquiring it by his own exertions. He may be a Brāhmaṇa, a Kṣatriya, a Vaiśya or a Śūdra. He should live either in a great city, or in a small town, or in the suburbs, or in a place inhabited by good people. He should have a house, big or small, according to his means; but as a fashionable man he should have a house in two compartments, inner and outer, the inner for his family and the outer for his friends. It should be close to a sheet of water and have a garden attached. The compartments should have many rooms. In the drawing room of the outer compartment, there should be a bedstead and a sofa, a polished bed with two pillows, one at the head and the other at the foot. The side pillows of the Bengalis were not in use in ancient times. The bed should be concave in the middle, covered with a clean white sheet. Alongside the bedstead, there should be another, a little lower, similarly furnished. Just above the head, perhaps in a niche, there should be spread, a seat for the god of the Nāgarika; and a platform, something like a rack projecting from the wall, where to keep the residue of the ointment used at night, the garland, a small box containing wax and another with scents, lemon-skin and betel. On the ground there should be a spitoon. On the wall, there should be hanging from a bracket, a Vīṇā, a painting canvas, paint-box, some favourite book, and a garland of Amaranth (Jhiṇṭi). On the floor, not very far from the bedstead there should be spread a coverlet with bolsters. There should be boards for chess and dice put against the wall. Outside the room should be cages for birds. In a corner there should be a spinning wheel and tools for carpentry as playthings. In a shady grove of trees, there should be an ordinary swing and another swinging round, and also seats covered over with flowers.

The daily duties of a Nāgarika.

He should rise early, perform his daily functions, rinse his teeth, thinly smear his person with ointment, perfume it with burning incense, wear garlands, paint his lips with wax and red-paint, chew *pān* with scent, stand before the mirror, then go about his business.

His other duties are: bathing every day, cleaning his body with perfumes every second day, softening his legs with Phenaka (something like soaps), shave the upper part of the body every fourth day and the lower part every fifth or tenth day. All this should be done with perfection. He should so behave that his armpits do not sweat. He should have two meals, one at forenoon and another in the afternoon. But Cārāyaṇa, the author of "Sāmānyādhikaraṇa" says, he should have one in the evening instead of in the afternoon. In "Mṛchhakaṭika," we find there is a tiffin early in the morning called Kalyavarta. That is neither in Cārāyaṇa nor in Vātsyāyana. And Cārāyaṇa wrote only a Sāmānyādhikarṇa. This may be an argument that Mṛcchakaṭika was composed even before Cārāyaṇa wrote. After his meal he should make his parrots talk. Then he sees cock-fight and the butting of rams and engages him in other diversions mentioned in the list of fine-arts. Then come his love-agents and associates in his intrigues. After dismissing them he takes a short nap. After the nap he dresses himself and goes to company. Then comes music at dusk. A little later he waits for his lady-loves in his well-furnished room, scented with burning incense, or sends out messengers to them or goes to meet them himself. When the ladies come, they are entertained with pleasant and flattering talk. If their dresses are drenched in rain, they are to be re-dressed with his own hands.

The Nāgarika is to organise all sorts of festivities at all the different seasons and all the year round. There are festive days for particular deities in the Hindu Calendar. And the fashionable men are to go to temples and organize festivities there. If wandering theatrical companies come, he is not only to look after their comforts but also to see that they are put to no difficulty, to help in their diseases and distress and also to see that they get reward for their skill in the art. The temple of Sarasvatī usually situated at a convenient distance from the inhabited quarters of the city, was generally the resort of the fashionable men on the fifth day of the waxing moon in the month of Māgha. The day is still celebrated throughout India as Vasanta-Pañcamī, and in Bengal as Sarasvatī-Pūjā. The organization of these and other pleasure parties used to be called Ghaṭā.

Occasional Duties.

There were *conversazionnes* in which people of the same age and of the same profession joined with fashionable women and talked of art, poetry etc. These may be held in their own houses, in the assembly-halls or also in the houses of the fashionable women.

There were carousals in which drinks of all sorts with all kinds of appetisers were used. These were generally held in the houses of the fashionable men by rotation, the women drinking and making other people drink.

Picnic : A number of Nāgarikas would go on horseback, gorgeously dressed, with women to gardens in the morning. There they would eat and drink, amuse and divert themselves with cock-fight, gambling, acting and other pleasant occupations, and then return home with trophies. In summer, they may sport in water after driving away dangerous aquatic animals.

Sports : There were three occasions for holding sports, the new moon of the month of Kārtika, the full moon of month of Kārtika, the full moon of the month of Āśvina ; and the advent of the spring is also regarded as one. People used to be wildly festive on these three occasions. They sang, they danced, they swung, they gambled, they played their musical instruments, and they sported themselves to their hearts' content. They had also their country sports, such as, pounding mangoes, burning corn and eating the grain, eating lotus-tendrils, running about on soft grass at the advent of the rains, a procession in the form used in the Pāñcāla country, sporting with flowers under a silk cotton tree, fighting with the Kadamba flowers at the advent of the rains. There are other sports too numerous to describe.

This is the picture of the life of a fashionable man in the first century A. D. in all parts of India, especially in Magadha, where the book was written. Times were not so hard as now. Any man with energy could acquire competence after a few years' labour and then give reins to the enjoyment of the good things of the world. Their days were passed in a pleasant routine and the years in a round of festivities. What wonder is there, that they should undertake to write a book like Kāmaśāstra on the physical and mental enjoyments.

I shall give you another picture of what a wife should be, from the fourth book in which Vātsyāyana has abridged the work of Gonardīya. A wife should have a single-minded devotion to her husband, she should keep her husband's secrets and should always serve him like a god. She should take upon herself the management of the household with the tacit consent of her husband. She should keep the house, sweep it clean, decorate it with flowers, make it bright and polished, pleasing to the eye, with offerings for three sacrifices, morning, noon and evening and with a neat and clean shrine for gods. Nothing, says Gonarda, is more charming for a householder than this. She should behave towards her superiors towards her servants, towards their husband's sisters and their husbands as befits her and as befits them. She is to prepare on clean ground, beds for green vegetables, for sugarcanes, for cumin seeds, for mustard, Joyān (Yavānī). In the garden she should plant all sorts of flowers used in worship, plants that flower in all seasons and Uśira, the fragrant grass. She should also prepare beautiful seats here and there. She should excavate wells, tanks and ponds. She should avoid the company of beggar women, Buddhist and Jaina nuns, women of indifferent character, juggleresses, female fortune-tellers and witches. She should know what food is liked by her husband and what is not; what is good to his health and what is not. When the husband is coming she should, on hearing his voice from outside, remain ready at home reflecting on what was to be done. She should wash the feet of her husband herself, sending away the maid-servant. She should never appear before her husband undressed and undecorated. If he is spending lavishly or spending for evil purposes, she should remonstrate with him in secret If she has to go to marriage parties, to sacrifices, to picnics with her friends or to temples of gods, she should do so with the permission of her husband. In all sports and amusements she should follow the bent of the mind of her husband. She should sleep after her husband is asleep, she should not awaken him when asleep. She should make the kitchen neat and clean and well-guarded At offences given by her husband she might be a little perturbed but should not protest loudly. She may, if necessary, use strong language, when he is alone or in the midst of his intimate friends; but never should she try to enchant him. For, nothing, says Gonarda, leads to distrust more than this. She should avoid angry words, angry looks and turning away while speaking. She should not long remain at the door, nor should she be looking out through it. She should not speak to others outside the house. And she should not remain long in any solitary place. She should understand that sweat, filth and bad smell cause annoyance. In approaching her husband, she should be well-decorated, well-perfumed in her body and well-dressed. When going out she should have a few ornaments, have not much of unguent and should have a plain simple silk dress and white flowers. She should follow her husband in all his fasts and vows. When asked to desist, she should say, " Do not insist in this matter". She should buy at the proper season and with the proper price, all vessels made of earth, wicker-work, wood, leather and metals. She should know how to keep concealed in the house things difficult to procure, such as, salt, oil, scent, good vessels and drugs. She should collect the seeds and plant them in their proper time. The passage runs thus :—Mūlakā-luka-pālaṅkī damanakāmrā-takair Vāruka-trapusa-vārtāka-kuṣmāṇḍālābu-suraṇa-śukanāsāḥ svayaṃ guptā tilaparṇikāgnimantha-laśuna-palāṇḍuprabhṛtīnāṃ sarvauṣadhīnāṃ ca vījagrahaṇam kāle vāpaś-ca.

She should not speak about her husband's treasure, nor about his secrets to others. She should excel her equals in her skill in fine-arts, in her high-mindedness and in her devoted service to her husband and in cooking. She should make an estimate of her husband's income and spend accordingly. With the surplus of milk she should prepare ghee. From mustard seeds and sugarcane she should prepare oil and molasses. She is to learn spinning and weaving. She should collect barks for the preparation of various kinds of strings She is to learn husking, cleaning, and how to superintend. She should utilize the gruels, husks, particles and scums of rice and charcoal. She should know the wages of the servants and their feeding. She should know all the processes of agriculture and the breeding of cattle and should look after the horses and other conveyances. She should look after the tending of sheep, cocks, fighting birds, she-parrots, cuckoos, peacocks, monkeys and deer. She should keep an eye on daily income and expenditure. She should keep together all old and new clothings, dye them in a variety of colours and grant them as rewards to servants for their good work or as presents to others. She should keep jars of wine and of liquor concealed, use them in time, look after purchases and sales, incomes and expenditure.

She should entertain and honour according to their position, her husband's friends with betels, garlands and unguents. Attendance to her husband's parents, entire dependence on them, not bandying words with them, speaking low and sparingly, not laughing loud, deporting herself to their friends and enemies as her own friends and enemies, not to be puffed up with wealth, liberality to her subordinates—these are the qualities which make a woman the ornament of her house. She should not give anything to anybody without the knowledge of her husband. She should employ the servants in their own work and reward them at the time of festivals.

Lecture V.

Vātsyāyana Bhāṣya

There is anothar Vātsyāyana who did signal service to Indian Literature by fixing the terminology and language of philosophical writings. He is, if not *the*, at least one of the earliest writers on philosophical subjects. All before him was in Sūtras and in mnemonic verses. From his time easy prose became the language of the higher thought. His work is the first of the Bhāṣya class, reducing the sūtras in ordinary language, explaining the views of the authors clearly and then giving his own criticism. Bhāṣyas before him were, so to say, independent treatises, see for instance, the Nirukta, the Bhāṣya on Nīghaṇṭu and the Mahābhāṣya of Patanjali on Pāṇini. Kauṭilya made a Bhāṣya on his own sūtras of Arthaśāstra, and therefore in his case the element of criticism can not be present.

It is said that Vātsyāyana's Bhāṣya on Nyāyasūtras is very difficult to understand and it appears rather strange that the writer whose avowed object was to bring philosophy within the comprehension of ordinary mortals and whose style, so lucid and so beautiful, should be regarded as difficult to understand. The difficulty is not in the Bhāṣya, it is in the sūtras. The sūtras are a patch-work. In their compilation and in their revision the working of several hands is clearly visible. The object of these revisions and interpolations is not always the advancement of the science, but the interest of parties. And Vātsyāyana had before him the difficult task of reducing this heterogenous mass into a harmonious system. That is the reason why he is often obscure and it cannot be asserted that his Bhāṣya, too, has not been tampered with in party interest.

But to understand his difficulties and to appreciate his services, it is necessary to give a history of the compilation of the sūtras in general, and of the Nyāya sūtras in particular. The Vedic sūtras, the Śrauta, the Gṛhya the Dharmasūtras were over in the sixth century B. C. The Sikṣā, Vyākaraṇa and other sūtras of the Aṅgas ended with Pāṇini, Piṅgala and their followers. The sūtras on subjects of ordinary concern in human affairs ended perhaps with the Kāmasūtras of Vātsyāyana Then came the philosophical sūtras. But sūtra or no sūtra, the philosophical speculations were there from seventh and sixth centuries B. C. or earlier.

There was a great upheaval of Indian mind in the seventh and sixth centuries B. C. and perhaps earlier. There seem to have been no internal or external war to disturb the peace of India. And the higher classes, especially the Brahmanas, devoted the entire energy of their mind to the advancement of thought, moral, spiritual, social, economic and so on. It was in fact an all round advancement. Every one aspired to say something new, to solve some difficult problem, to add something to the extent of human knowledge, to alleviate and assuage some suffering and to do something to make life tolerable and pleasant. Everyone ran with some new idea and there was so much of preaching and so much of propaganda work. If we look into the Upaniṣads, the latest effusions of the Vedic age and the writings of the early

Buddhists and Jainas one thing that strikes us, as strange, is the enormous number of names of authors or teachers. Each of them had to say something,—a new idea, a dogma, a precept, a concept,—something to add to our knowledge, something made more systematic, more clear and more refined. In the early Upaniṣads (Vedic) even the five organs of perception and five organs of work were not well known, for we often meet with such expressions in Taittirīya and other older Upaniṣads as—Cakṣuḥ, śrotraṃ, manaḥ, vāk, tvak, and Annaṃ, prāṇaḥ, cakṣuḥ śrotraṃ.

It is from these primitive notions that we reach in the phisophical sūtras to refined classifications and subtle distinctions. The process is long, tedious and full of difficulties and had taken many centuries. Scholars are apt to say that the seeds of the philosophical sūtras were to be found in the literature of the upheaval. But this is rather misleading. The accurate way of saying would be that the various topics dealt with in the sūtras are to be found in a primitive form — in a germinal stage in the literature of those days. Some of these topics have been traced with considerable ability by the Japanese scholar Mr. UI, in the introduction to the Vaiśeṣika Philosophy according to the Daśapadārthī Sūtra. Four elements in the Upaniṣads were, Mahābhūtas and as such not atomic. Pakuda Kaccayana, one of the six heritical teachers of the Budhists, says that Earth, Fire, Water and Air; pleasure, pain and soul are neither made, nor caused to be made and that they are barren. This is not yet atomic. But he held body and things have the same quantity of elements but they are not same in appearance; to reconcile this distinct contradiction an atomic theory may suit better than any other, and it also appears as a natural consequence Jainas maintain that everything in this world except the soul and mere space is produced from matter (pudgala) and that all matter consists of atoms or *Paramāṇus*. Matter, however, may be in a gross state or in a subtle state, innumerable atoms occupy the space of one gross atom. Atoms are eternal as regards their substances, each atom has one kind of taste, smell and colour and two kinds of touch. The qualities however, are not permanent and fixed for several atoms but they may be changed and developed in them. The Vaiśeṣika system of atoms is more advanced than this. It has different kinds of atoms corresponding to the four elements, while in the Jaina system the atoms are only of one kind. Thus Mr. UI has carefully collected from the Indian and Chinese sources the conditions and modifications of the atomic theory in all its various stages from the Upaniṣads to the Vaiśeṣika sūtras. It is a very interesting investigation and repays perusal. It is possible similarly to trace the development of every theory from its inception in 6th and 7th centuries B.C. to the period of the philosophic sūtras.

As I have already said, we would look in vain for the origin of the sūtras in the period of the upheaval. But if we look for the origin of the various topics treated of in the sūtras, we are likely to meet with better success These various topics were started early and criticised, remodelled and refined. Each school took such topics as it wanted and in such form as it wanted. Various schools were formed, some were short-lived like the Kālakāraṇikas, Īśvarakāraṇikas, Arthacintakas, others remained for centuries to influence human thought and then disappeared, such as Ājīvakas, Celakas, Parivrājakas and others. Some have come down to us and their traditional number is six. But the number six is variously counted ; Bauddha, Ārhata, Vaiśeṣika, Sāṃkhya,

Mimāṃsa and Nyāva is one way of counting six. If you want to introduce Lokāyata, omit Nyāya, which is akin to Vaiśeṣika. The modern counting enumerates another group of six, namely, Pūrva and Uttara Mīmāṃsās. Sāṃkhya and Yoga; Nyāya and Vaiśeṣika. There is another group of six Brahma, Īśvara, Bauddha, Ārhata, Sāṃkhya and Lokāyata. So there are several groups according to the time and taste of the writers.

So there was a time when these ideas were mooted in Indian Sceiety. They were criticised and refined. They were grouped for the purpose of forming schools and systematized. The sūtras were compiled sometime later. So if an investigation is to be made into the origin of these sūtra works, one has to begin with the various *adhikaraṇas* or single-topics which compose the sutra work

This is the general history of the development of philosophic thought in India. In dealing with Vātysyāyana's Bhāṣya we have much to do with the heterodox systems of the Buddhists and Jainas and Saṃkara stigmatises the Vaiśeṣika system as Ardhavaināśika or Half-Nihilist, while the Buddhists were Nihilists pure and simple and it is supposed in many quarters to have been unorthodox. The savant who composed the sūtra took a number of adhikaraṇas from the current thought of the time, interpreted them in his own way and stringed them together into Ahnikas and Adhyāyas. Nyāya follows the footsteps of the Vaiśeṣikas only giving more attention to Logic than to Physics and Metaphysics. Some history, therefore, of the systems will be useful in understanding and appreciating the work of Vātsyāyana.

The earliest system studied and investigated in India is the Vedānta system as taught in the Upaniṣads. But Upaniṣads were long regarded as a part of the Brāhmaṇas and used in Karma Kāṇḍa and so they were kept within

Brahmānic circle. The distinction between Jnānakāṇḍa and Karmakānda came in very late. So the philosophy of the Upaniṣads remained, so to say, in abeyance and did not develop till the sixth century A. D. In the seventh we hear in Harṣacarita of a school of Aupaniṣadas,[1] *i.e.*, who studied Upaniṣads as a school of Philosophy, giving rise in later centuries to the Vedāntins. So the oldest thought in India developed the latest.

Next to Vedanta comes Sāṃkhya, the enumerative philosophy, the attempt to fix ideas by numbers and in fact in the Kapila Sūtras, 22 in number, almost every sūtra contains a number, thus showing that the word Sāṃkhya is significant. But the age of these 22 sūtras is not certain. They show much advanced ideas, such as Tripramāṇa, which may be later than that of Nyāya. Scholars are unanimous in thinking that the earliest work of Sāṃkhya extant is the 70 Kārikās of Iśvarakṛṣṇa. There are three more Kārikās giving the succession of teachers and other historical information about the school. These say that there was a work entitled Saṣṭitantra, one chapter of which treated of the opinions of other schools and another of the stories. Now there is a work in six chapters known as Sāṃkhya Pravacana one chapter of which contains refutation of the doctrines of the other schools from a Sāṃkhya point of view and another chapter treats of stories of votaries who attained Siddhi easily by Sāṃkhya practices. But scholars are again unanimous in rejecting the claim of the Sāṃkhya Pravacana as an old body of sūtras. They say that the work is full of Vedānta ideas and was composed by Vijñāna-Bhikṣu, the author of the Bhāṣya who belonged to the 11th or 12th century and was a follower of Saṃkara. I have found a sūtra from the

---

[1] Bom. Sans ; Series Harṣacarita p. 316, l. 9.

Saṣṭitantra in Gauḍapāda's Bhāṣya on the 70 kārikās [1] but unfortunately that sūtra is not to be found in the Sāmkhya Pravacana Sūtras. The Pravacana might have been based on the Saṣṭi-tantra but it has been so much altered by later modifications as to be beyond recognition.

So the oldest work on Sāṃkhya extant is the collection of 70 Kārikās by Īsvarakṛṣṇa written in the 5th century of the Christian Era or earlier. But there were collections of sūtras, the existence of one of which called the Saṣṭitantra is vouched by the Kārikās themselves. The meaning of the word Saṣṭitantra is involved in obscurity but a modern commentator, Nārāyana, has boldly cut the Gordian knot by declaring that the work contained sixty topics and by giving the names of the topics. But we know of another school of Sāṃkhya which the Bhagavat-Gītā and the Kaṭhopaniṣad explain; it believes in Mahattattva coming between Avyakta and Buddhi. Asvaghoṣa in his Budha-caritā speaks of the Buddhist idea of Nirvāṇa as an advance on the Sāṃkhya doctrines and his system is the same as that of Bhagavat-Gīta and Kaṭhopaniṣad. Going to certain grounds we find Sāṃkhya being named as a school of thought by Kauṭilya in the 4th century B.C. This is all that is known of the ancient Sāṃkhya literature before Īsvarakṛṣṇa. The Parivrājakas were the oldest school of wandering ascetics in India much older than the Buddhists and the Jainas. Guṇaratna in his commentary on Haribhadra's Saḍdarsana Samuccaya says that these were the followers of Sāṃkhya. (P. 95, Bibl. Ind. Edition).

There is no doubt that the Sāmkhya System got its name from Sāṃkhyā or number. It appears to have been

---

[1] तथचोक्तं षष्टितंत्रं "पुरुषाधिष्ठितं पधानं प्रवर्तते"
Çomm : Gauḍ : Kārikā 17.

older even than Buddhism which it has profoundly influenced. Some think that Buddhism is a direct outcome of Sāṃkhya and early Buddhism is full of Saṃkhyā; *Four* Noble Truths, *Twelve* Āyatanas, *Five* Skandhas and so on. Buddhism, for a long time stuck to enumeration, so much so, that they taught little boys, numbers by concepts.

As I have told you the earliest method of controlling higher thought was by fixing the concepts by number. The thoughts were fleeting, vanishing and difficult to fix in the mind and still more difficult to impart and the best way to deal with them was to number them. But when they became too many and when the sphere of thought expanded it became necessary to invent another method and that method was *comparison* to find similarities and dissimilarities among concepts fixed by number for the purpose of classification and this is afforded by the Vaiseṣik Sūtras in which Sādharmya and Vaidharmya was the key-note. Throughout the work the idea is similarity and dissimilarity. In fact the special characteristics of the system are Samānya and Viseṣa, Generalisation and particularisation or differentiation. It has got its name Vaiseṣika from particularisation. Take a number of things, go on finding similarities or Sādharmaya till you come to something which you can predicate to all the things. This is the highest similarity. Then again, find dissimilarities and come to the ultimate analysis to individualities, the lowest of dissimilarities. In this way classifying and analysing all the numenon and phenomenon of the world, Kaṇāda comes to the ultimate generalisation Pura-Sāmānya *i. e.*, existence Sattā and the ultimate differentiation that is Viseṣa. Between these ultimates lie all phenomena to which both similarity and dissimilarity can be predicated.

The History of the Vaiseṣika Sūtras also have a

chequered life. It is traditionally affirmed that it had eighteen schools.[1] It is not known how far the tradition is correct. But recently comes from China a school of Vaiśeṣika with ten categories. It is also well known that what it called the Praśasta Bhāṣya is but an independent treatise differing in many material points from the sūtras, so it may be a Bhāṣya of the old style which amplified and criticised the original. The editor of Praśastapāda points out that 53 sūtras have been omitted[2] altogether and that the Bhāṣyakāra adopted an order of treatment of the subject which is quite different from that in the sūtras. There is another school called the Saptapadārthī, which, though comparatively modern appears to be based on an old one because the moderns have not the boldness to start a new school unless they have some old school to rely upon.

Saṃkarācāryya calls even Sāṃkhya unorthodox. He condescended to criticise it because certain orthodox people like Manu adopted it. The treatment of Vaiśeṣika in his hands is more drastic; he calls it Ardha-Vaināśika, half Nihilistic. He knew that it had a heterodox origin though it was regarded as orthodox because the Kaṇāda Sūtras often appeal to the Vedas and Āgamas. The Sūtra from China makes no such appeal. Kaṇāda has put in a chapter on the Vedas and defends Vedic rituals. For these reasons Vaiśeṣika is regarded as othodox in modern times.

The progress of philosophical methods from enumeration to comparison is represented by the systems of Sāṃkhya and Vaiśeṣika. Then come arguments and discussion, that is, Nyāya, often mistranslated as Logic. The Nyāya-sūtra begins with Pramāṇa and ends with points defeat in argument. There is much in the sūtras which is outside the

---

[1] Ui. preface.

[2] Last page, preface, Benares Ed.

province of Logic. Our forefathers used to call the Nyāya sūtras, Tarkaśāstra. That should be its proper name,—the art of descussion. Examine the sixteen categories of Nyāya All of them relate to discussion. (1) Pramaṇa, the means by which we can discriminate which is true, (2) Prameya, that which is ascertained by true knowledge, (3) Saṃśaya, doubt, (4) Prayojana, object, (5) Dṛṣṭānta, examples, (6) Siddhānta, doctrine, (7) Avayava, syllogism, (8) Tarka, attempt to find the truth in unknown subjects by argument, (9) Nirṇaya, finding the truth, (10) Vāda, finding out truth honestly by hearing both sides, (11) Jalpa, establishing one's own position by defeating the adversary, (12) Vitaṇḍā, defeating the adversary without establishing one's own position, (13) Hetvābhāsa, false reasoning (14), Chala, quibbling, (15) Jāti, futility, (16) Nigrahasthāna, points of defeat. All these relate to one object, namely discussion. There were Parṣads all over the Aryan world. The learned men of the locality formed the Parṣad. They had to decide all sorts of cases, civil and criminal. They had to interpret Śāstras. They had to decide between the various schools of thought. The Tarkaśāstra is really a guide book to the Parṣads. The Privy Council of the king used to be called the Mantri-Pariṣad. So wherever it was necessary to decide between man and man, there was a Pariṣad or Parṣad and there were some rules. The last Chapter of Kauṭilya, named Tantrayukti gives some of the rules. If the Nyāyasūtra was logic pure and simple, the points of defeat, Nigrahasthāna, would have no place in it. One rule is, if a party remains silent after he is called upon to reply by the Pariṣad three times he is defeated. This is no part of logic. But the rule is necessary in a work for the guidance of discussion. There were other guide books before these sūtras were composed, for, in the Kathāvatthu

composed in the Third Council of the Buddhists held at Pāṭaliputra in the 17th year of Aśoka, the system of conducting controversy was quite different. In that work, called in English, Points of Controversy, the first point is given in full detail. But in that detailed description of a controversy there is not a word about syllogism. The Mīmāṁsa method of conducting controversy also was different.—
Viśayo Viṣayaścaiva pūrvapakṣastathottaraḥ.
Nirṇayaśceti pañcāṅgaṃ Śāstre dhikaraṇaṃ Smṛtaṁ.
The Saptabhaṅgī Nyaya of the Jainas and the Catuṣkoṭi, sat, asat, sadasat and nāsat-na-sat of the Buddhists are different methods of discussion. As I have said before, this sūtra is a book for the guidance of Parṣads. Philosophy has but a secondary importance in it. In fact in the first sūtra giving the topics to be treated of there, not a word of metaphysical or epistemological or of ethical importance, is to be found. They have been introduced under the head of Prameya. But Prameya is a subject absolutely necessary in a book for the guidance of judges. The metaphysical and other topics, if expunged, it would not in the least, detract from its value as a book on Tarkaśāstra. In fact, I think, all these topics are interpolations and I will now try to show how these interpolations came in.

Originally it was an unsectarian work which could be used by all classes of men like the Auther of the Arthaśāstra and that of the Kāmasūtra but it was a very small work, the First Book with a few sūtras omitted. The commentators say that all philosophical sūtras have three parts, Uddeśa, Lakṣaṇa, and Parīkṣā, enumeration, definition and examination or criticism. The enumeration of topics is given in the first sūtra, the definitions are spread over the first chapter. But the examination is neither systematic nor exhaustive. If systematic, one would expect that Pramāṇa would be examined first, but no; the first topic examined is Saṃśaya. Then come the Pramāṇas, four in number and then Prameyas. The last two heads Jāti and Nigrahasthāna occupy the whole of the Fifth Book.

The Fifth Chaper has two Ahnikas, one gives the names of Jātis or futilities in argument and the other Nigrahasthāhas, points of defeat Yet they do not seem to be written by one man. For Matānujñā is described as a subdivision of Jāti in the first Ahnika, and the same Matānujñā is also described as one of the points of defeat. If one man wrote both, he, could not have given the same technical name in a philosophical sūtra to two objects so dissimilar in nature. These lists seem to have been old lists coming down from generation to generation and having therefore acquired a traditional veneration. These are like appendices to the First Chapter of Nyāya Sūtra for while defining Jāti and Nigrahasthāna, in the First Chapter the author seem to have done with them For he gave all the sub-divisions of Hetvābhāsa and Chala. in book I, but in the case of Jāti and Nigrahasthāna, he simply said that they are many. So he really finished with them. If you say, in the Fifth Chapter, the writer simply expanded the meaning of the word 'many' there will be another serious difficulty. The term Prakaraṇasama is one of the Hetvābhāsas. The same Prakaraṇasama is again one of the Jātis. The writer who can use the same technical term for two things in the same philosophical work is not deserving of credit. But if he does so again and again, he is still more undeserving of credit. Therefore, to save the reputation of the author of the Nyāyasūtra it is better to call the two Ahnikas of the Fifth Chapter as appendices in which old lists have been incorporated.

In all other philosophical sūtras the enumeration of

topics is generally given in one sūtra and the object of the whole work stated there. But in Nyāya we have a second Sūtra. The topics enumerated there—in that sūtra has nothing to do either with logic or with regulation of discussion. All the topics there are metaphysicial in the highest degree. They are—misery, transmigration, hankering, fault and false knowledge and emancipation. Why after the full enumeration of all the topics necessary for Tarkaśāstra, there should be necessary a second sūtra of a metaphysical nature is a puzzle and Vātsyāyana wants to solve it by saying that Niḥśreyasa in the first sūtra means a knowledge of self-emancipation and the second sūtra is necessary to record the steps by which that emancipation is to be attained. The explanation is not satisfactory. His commentator Uddyotakara does not take the word Niḥśreyasa in the sense of spiritual knowledge alone but in a more extended meaning. He says that Ministers, Generals, Merchants and even ordinary men may attain Niḥśreyasa, the highest prosperity in their respective lines by the study of these Tarka topics. So he does not confine himself to spiritual attainment alone. I suspect that the second sūtra was put in by some one before Vātsyāyana who wanted to give this non-sectarian book on Tarka or Logic a sectarian or metaphysical turn and there were in those days many sects who held different views in metaphysical subjects. If Vatsyāyana did not introduce the sūtra himself, he took upon himself to defend it and to give the whole work a metaphysical interpretation, and he became in fact the founder of a school on metaphysics, which has at the present moment given rise to several sects.

It may not be out of place to mention here that the Second Sūtra in Nayāya sūtras smells of Buddhist paticca-samuppāda. Avijjāppaccayā saṃkhārā, saṃkhārappaccayā-

Viññāṇāñī, Viññāṇappaccayonāmarūpaṃ, nāmarūpappaccayā ṣaḍāyatanāni, saḍāyatanappaccayā phaṃso, phaṃsappaccayā vedanā, vedunāppaccūya tanhā, tanhāppaccayo bhabo, bhavappaccayo jāti, jatippaccayā jārāmaraṇ-śoka—parideva-dukkha-domanassāpāyādi bhavanti.

I will now explain how the introduction of that sūtra has changed the whole aspect of the work. The topics there cannot be included in any one of the topics of the first sūtra except prameya and in the lakṣaṇa or description of prameya these have been put in at the end. See the 9th sūtra—

"Ātma-Śarīr-endriya-buddhi-manaḥ pravṛtti-doṣa-pretya-phala-duhkhāpavargāḥ Prameyaṃ."

The first six are acknowledged as prameyas by almost all the sects. The last six came from the second sūtra with a slight change of names in one or two cases. The sūtras 17, 18, 19, 20, 21 and 22 define the objects mentioned in that sūtra.

Now, let us come to the examination or parikṣā of these sūtras. The examination of saṃśaya, pramāṇa and the first six items of prameya take up the second and the third adhyāyas. The other six items occupy the first āhnika of the fourth chapter ending with metaphysical tattvajñāna and emancipation. The other ahnika improves tattvajñāna. So this whole chapter has nothing to do with logic or a guide to discussion. If, however, the second sūtra and its appendages are removed the whole work will be rules for discussion and I think, this conversion of a book on logic to a book on metaphysics we owe to a Buddhist savant. Tattvajñāan is not a category, not one of the sixteen, then why it should be examined at all and why at such length? As I have said before, the orthodox people were not much in favour of Tarkaśāstra. Manu hates Hetuśāstra which is another name of

Tarkaśāstra ; so this was at one time the peculiar property of the heretics, Buddhists and others.

Nāgārjuna believed in four pramāṇas. This śāstra, too, believes in four pramāṇas. The four pramāṇas are defined in four sūtras 4, 5, 6 and 7. Then uncalled for comes another sūtra 8. "Sa (śabdaḥ) dīvidhaḥ dṛṣṭādṛṣṭārthatvāt. The object of introducing this sūtra appears expanded in the examination of pramāṇas where there is a long discussion on the authenticity of the Vedas But in this matter the interpolator, whoever he is, opposes the Mīmāṃsakas who believe in the eternity of sound. Thus the work was made not only metaphysical but brahmanic, and therefore, orthodox.

In the beginning of the lecture, I called the Nyāyasūtra a patch-work, and I have now proved that the two ahnikas of the Fifth Chapter are by two men, and that they are different from the writer of the First Chapter and that in the First Chapter there are at least two interpolations made by two authors with two distinct objects. The second ahnika of the Fourth Chapter, too, appears to be strange, for it treats of tattvajñāna which is not a category and stranger still it treats of the increase of tattvajñāna. I think, I am justified in calling it a patchwork. But if the sūtras are a patch-work, the task of making the patch-work a homogenous whole is a very difficult work and let us now see how Vātsyāyana has done his work.

Vātsyāyana was conscious of what he was doing—that he was introducing a spiritual significance into something which is not exactly spiritual. But he has no hesitation, no prevarication; he goes straight to say that it is a spiritual science, but not purely spiritual. He says—Seyaṃ ānvīkṣikī, pramāṇādibhiḥ padārthair vibhajyamānā,—

Pradīpaḥ sarvvavidyānāmupāyaḥ sarvakarmaṇāṃ.

Aśrayaḥ sarvadharmāṇāṃ Vidyoddeśe prakīrtitā. Tadidam tattvajñānam niḥśreyasādhigamārtham yathāvidyam veditavyam. Ihāto adhyātmavidyāyām ātmāditattvajñānam, niḥśreyasādhigamopavarga-prāptiḥ.

"This science, ānvīkṣikī, divided into categories pramāṇa and others becomes the lamp of all sciences, the means of all undertakings, and the refuge of all law as said in the Chapter entitled Vidyoddeśa" (or Vidyāsamuddeśa in the Arthaśāstra of Kauṭilya). Therefore, this true knowledge is, according to the śāstra (you study) for the purpose of the highest good. But here in this spiritual science, the true knowledge is that Ātmā etc. and the highest good is emancipation.

He boldly declares the sole object of the śāstra to be attainment of spiritual excellence, but at the same time he says that the porfessors of other sciences may also benefit by it. (Commentary on the First Sutra, at the end). In another place he says "That the Nyāya-vidyā has struck a new path inasmuch as it has taken doubt etc., as categories. Unless they were separately spoken of, this would be a mere spiritual science like the Upaniṣads. (P. 4, Jīvānanda's Edition). The doubt and the rest of the categories, if not separately enumerated, but included as they ought to have been, in the second category, prameya, the science would be mere Adhyātmya-vidyā.

Tattvajñāna, he defines—Sat sat iti gṛhyamāṇaṃ yathabhūtam aviparītaṃ tattvaṃ bhavati. Asat ca asat ili gṛhyamāṇaṃ yathābhūtam aviparītaṃ tattvaṃ bhavati.

"When entity is taken as entity, as it is, and not contradicted, it is thatness *Tattvā* and when non-entity is taken as non-entity, as it is, and not contradicted that also is *Tattva*." This is so like the Buddhist *Tathatā*. The next quotation, too, smells of Buddhism—Heyaṃ tasya nivarttakaṃ hānam ātyayitikaṃ tasyopāyo dhigantavyaḥ ityetāni catvāri arthapadāni. Samyak buddhvā niḥsreyasamadhigacchati.

Is it not the same as the Four Noble Truths—

"Ye dharmā hetuprabhavā hetuntesāṃ Tathāgatohyavadat;

Tesāñca yo nirodho evam vādī mahāñsramaṇaḥ," and the Dukkham, Dukkha-saumdayo, Dukkha-nirodho and Dukkhanirodhagāiminī paṭipat, of the Mahāyāna and of the Pali Buddhism? Even Vātsyāyana, who has made the Nyāyasāstra Brāhmaṇic, and orthodox metaphysics, sails close to Buddhism. The Nyāyasūtra wants to prove the prameya, the object of knowledge both subjective and objective from pramāṇas, proofs. The Buddhists say how do you establish your proofs themselves? The Nyāya-sūtra says like lamps, they illuminate themselves. Nāgārjuna in one of his works says "No, the lamp can illuminate others in the dark, but it cannot illuminate itself." (Ui, Introduction, page 5). This shows that Nāgārjuna is later than the Nyāya Sūtra. But Nyāya sūtra attacks Śūnyavāda of Nāgārjuna and therefore, Mr. UI comes to the conclusion that the sūtra and Nāgārjuna must be contemporaries and so refute each other. Mr. UI is right so far as he goes. But I have established the fact that the whole of the sūtra is not the work of one man, but of six men, at least, at six different times. Nāgārjuna may refute one of the earlieer works, namely, that containing the first chapter minus the interpolations and the greater part of the second and third chapter. But I am afraid the fourth chapter in which Śūnyatā and Vāhyārthabhaṅga are dealt with is not written by the same author. That chapter may be later than Nāgārjuna, because it also refutes such late theories as Īsvarakāraṇika. As the work is by different hands it is useless to attempt to fix the date of its composition. It is sufficient to say that the whole book was compiled between 200 B.C. and 300 A.D.

And therefore I now propose to dwell upon the services of Vātsyāyana to the philosophic literature of India. He has made the heterogenous mass of sūtras compiled from the vast quantity of floating philosophical speculations of the period into a homogenous whole and given it a character and consistency which has lasted nearly 1600 years. On the one hand, he defended the system against the advocates of extreme idealism of the Mahāyāna Buddhists, like Nāgārjuna and Deva and on the other hand he defended it against the advocates of the extreme orthodox schools of the Brahmins. His common sense rebelled against the theory that the world was produced from void, and that what we see outside has no reality beyond the impressions left in our mind, as well as against the theory that sound was eternal, the Vedas were eternal and that the world was either eternal or all non-eternal and so on. He stood manfully in the midst of extremists, kept the evtremists of both sides at arm's length and vindicated common sense. He proved the authenticity of the Vedas, not by declaring that sound was eternal but in the ordinary way, because, the seers and speakers were reliable men. Just as you rely upon your physicians and doctors so you rely on the Ṛṣis. They have seen the law and they are most competent to advise and instruct in what to do and what not to do. But his greatest service is the establishment of God as a Personal God and as a Moral Governor. He is not an angry God nor a benevolent God but imparts justice tempered with mercy and dispenses rewards according to Karma. This is Vātsyāyana's own work, for the sūtra does not believe in a God and the section on rewards if read alone will produce an impression that the Nyāyasūtra is Nirīsvara *i.e.*, Godless ; but he explains the sūtras in a different way. There is no Īśvara in the categories. But he says there is Ātmā, one of these Ātmās is Īśvara, the possessor of eight supernatural powers, full of righteousness, full of true knowledge and full of concentration of mind. He can do whatever he wills, he sets in motion the inner workings of man and elements in their own work. He is father to the creatures, he is the seer, the Omnipotent and Omniscient. He is beyond comprehension of all creatures. In later literature he is Śiva and so Haribhadra says—

"Akṣapādanaye Devo sṛṣṭi saṃhārakṛt Śivaḥ.
Vibhurnityaikasarvajño nityabuddhisamāśrayaḥ."

And Śiva has remained the object of veneration of the Naiyāyikas even to the present day.

The services of Vātsyāyana are certainly great in Metaphysics and in Religion and his services are no less valuable in the matter of regulating the rules of discussion or vicāra. The proceedings settled by him in his Bhāṣya are still followed in all Hindu courts and controversies. The Madhyastha sits in the place of the Parṣad and hears both sides, weighs the arguments on both sides according to rules laid down by him and decides. The rules are also the same. The most important thing in an Anumāna is syllogism and the Nyāya Sūtra lays down that it should have five limbs. But there are some who discard two of them and reduce the number to three. Hence some people think that the Hindus have derived their form of syllogism from Aristoltle who belonged to the fourth century B.C. But this is not correct. For the limbs or parts of syllogism were at one time ten, for so says Vātsyāyana in his commentary on the Avayava Sūtra (I, i, 32) and he gives their names and functions and says that laterly they were considered superfluous and Mr. UI has shown in a note on p. 83 of his preface that

Bhadrabāhu who died in 293 B.C. elaborates a form of syllogism with ten members. These ten by later criticism were reduced to five So the Indians developed their syllogism independently of the Greeks. Vātsyāyaua has been vehemently criticised by Diṇnāga in the middle of the 5th century A.D. and so he must have lived sometime before Diṇnāga.

So the services of Vātsyāyana to Logic, Metaphysics and Religion of the Hindus are invaluable.

Lecture VI.

During the 5th Century of the Christian Era, when the Guptas were the masters of nearly the whole of India, there was in the Vātsyāyana family, a Vedic scholar named Kuvera of wide fame and deep learning. He was the master of all the sciences of his day and an expert in all sorts of sacrifices. He had four sons of whom the last was Paśupati; his son was Arthapati who performed innumerable secrifices. His son was Cittrabhānu who kept up the reputation of his ancestors by his learning and piety.[1] His son was Vāṇa. Vāṇa lost his mother early[2] and his fathers at fourteen.[3] Vāṇa received his education in his own family, but became very unruly and led a wild life. He went on travel. In his tour round Northern India he had a large following including dancers, actors, musicians, nuns etc. Though people admired him for his learning, his reputation for Brahmanic purity of life was not very great.[4] However, after some years of wild and roving life he become chastened.[5] On his return home he took his position as the head of the Vātsyāyana family which could then boast of many learned and highly cultured Brāhmaṇas. He took a great delight in Vedic sacrifices, both Śrauta

---

[1] Harsacarit, I para 25. Ed. Gajendra Godkr. [2] Ibid.
[3] Ibid para. 26. [4] Ibid. [5] Ibid para. 27.

and Smārta and in many of the fine-arts.[1] Once upon a time when after the day's work he was enjoying the cool breeze of the Śoṇa, a man came gallopping on horseback and alighting from his horse was introduced to him by his low-caste brother Candrasena, unfolded his turban,[2] handed him a letter. He read it with intense attention, as it was from Kṛṣṇagupta, the Prime-Minister of Harṣavardhana of Thāneśvara. Kṛṣṇagupta pointed out to him that this was a fine opportunity to seek an interview with the great Emperor.[3] Next morning Vāṇa prepared for the journey and in a few days came to where the emperor was in camp.[4] The encampment was of a vast dimension and Vāṇa describes it with a vividity and minuteness which would do honour to any poet of any country and of any age.

On entering the Imperial Court Kṛṣṇagupta beckoned to him to sit quietly close by, while he was conferring with the Emperor on state affairs. The conference was long and in whispers, which irritated Vāṇa very much. However, at the end of the conference Kṛṣṇagupta introduced Vāṇa to the Emperor who simply remarked "*Mahānayaṃ bhujaṅgaḥ.*"[5] The remark irritated Vāṇa most. The word means not only a serpent but also a "dandy" a "ladies' man." Vāṇa thought that the king railed at him for his behaviour during his tour, but Kṛṣṇagupta soon found an opportunity to soothe his irritation and in a short time Harṣa and Vāṇa were friends. Vāṇa's position in the Imperial Court was very high and he was very happy.[6]

After prolonged stay at the camp with the Emperor

---

[1] Ibid II, para, 1.
[2] Ibid II, para. 7.
[3] Ibid II, paras. 6 & 7.
[4] Ibid II, 10.
[5] Ibid II, 18.
[6] Ibid II, 19.

Vāṇa became anxious to be in the midst of his family and secured permission to visit his native place.[1] At home he found the whole family engaged in listening every evening to the recital of a *Pravamāna-prokta Purāṇa.*[2] A reciter of the Purāṇa came every evening, opened a palm-leaf manuscript, read out long passages from it and went away just before dusk to say his evening prayer. Among the attentive listeners were the four cousins of Vāṇa. One of them remarked after hearing the history of ancient kings in the Purāṇa "These kings of antiquity had but small territories, yet the Purāṇa records so much of their achievements and of their virtue. Our Emperor Harṣa has vast territories and he is so virtuous and popular. Why do you not, O Vāṇa, write a Purāṇa embodying an account of his work." Vāṇa nodded consent and began to write the Harṣacarita.[3]

Thus began in the early years of the Seventh Century a historical literature in India, which though not very fruitful in the beginning is now putting forth the best results. One of the reasons why it was not fruitful in the beginning is the unfortunate fact that Vāṇa did not live to finish his work. If he could have finished it, in his vigorous and inimitable style, others would certainly have followed in his wake. Because Vāṇa could not finish it, people thought that history was an inauspicious subject and by all means avoided it. The same was the case with the Kathā Literature which Vāṇa began with his Kādambarī, but which he could not finish. The Kathā Literature, therefore, did not flourish, though his worthy son Bhūṣana completed his work.

Vāṇa's Harṣacarita is the first historical work written in Sanskrit. In ancient India there were histories and

---

[1] III, 1. [2] Ibid III, 4. [3] Ibid III, 7.

I have already told you that history ranked as a Fifth Veda. But we get no historical works of that time. The only thing we get is the list of kings of the various dynasties that ruled in India, and in Magadha only we get along with the names the duration of each reign. Mr. Pargiter who has investigated the subject carefully, says that the lists were kept in Prakit. Be that as it may, there is no doubt that the men who prompted Vāṇa to write the Harṣacarita thought they were asking him to do something new. They were asking him to do for a modern king what the Purāṇas did for the ancient kings and Vāṇa did his work in the spirit of a modern Nineteenth or Twentieth century historian. He gives a history of his Gotra, then of his immediate ancestors to the 5th generation, and an autobiography of himself, and also the occasion which induced him to write the history of the king he served. In writing an account of his own life he did not paint himself as an immaculate person but painted himself as he was, without hiding any of his faults. He was an ardent admirer of the king but he has not spared his faults. In the true spirit of a historian he gives the history of the dynasty to which the king belonged. What he says about Pravākaravardhana, Rājyavardhana and Harṣavardhana is well known from the histories of India which have all exploited what historical information he has given. The book throws a flood of light on Indian life at the beginning of the 7th century A.D.

Vāṇa's Kādambarī is a tale, but it is a wonderful tale. It extends over three births of a number of its characters, there are words which are three four lines long and sentences, which run over four or five pages. One of my professors measured a sentence by a string in the old edition of the Kādambarī in very small type and the string was 36 ft. long. The story is a wonderful mixture of the Natural and the Supernatural. The moon becomes in one birth Tārāpīḍa, the Prince of Ujjain, and in another Śūdraka, the king of Vidiśā, and Punṇḍarika, the son of Laksmī becomes Vaiśampayana in one birth and in another-a parrot. The story resembles in many features the Pali Buddhist story of Śyāmāvatī translated into Bengali from Chittagong about 30 years ago. That story, too, goes through several transmigrations of the soul. The story of Kādambarī comes from that inexhaustible source of stories, the Vṛhatkathā of Guṇāḍhya now lost but represented by the Kathā-Sarit-Sāgara of Someśvara. The only other work of Vāṇa known is Caṇḍīśataka[1] which contains one hundred verses on goddess Durgā. Three Śatakas were written about that time. This one by Vāṇa, the Sūryyaśataka by his father-in-law, Mayūra, and the Bhaktā-marastotra by Mānatunga—the three Śatakas representing the three great religions flourishing side by side in the capital of Harṣa.

Vātsāyana the Physician.

The Pañcatantra names two physicians (i) Śālihotra and (ii) Vātsyāyana.[2] Śālihotra, the author of Aśva-śāstra was an inhabitant of Western Punjab. But Vātsyāyana certainly belonged to the family of Prītikūṭa on the banks of the Śoṇa. Modhusūdana Sarasvatī in his Prasthānabheda says that Kāmasūtra is a part of Ayurveda. From this Weber seems to think that Vātsyāyana the Physician mentioned in the Pañcatantra is the same as the author of Kāmaśāstra. From the mere mention of a name it is impossible to draw any inference. But I am inclined to think that there may

1 Printed in the Kāvyamāla Series.

2 See Webers Sanskrit Literature 166 & 267 and note.

have been a physician of the family of Vātsyāyana as the Gotra was a learned and an extensive one, and the period of their influence in Magadha extended over many centuries. The author of the Pañcatantra which was translated into Pehlevi under orders of Khusru Nauservan in the 6th century A.D knew more of the Vātsyāyana family than we in the 20th century and even Vāṇa in the 7th century. Madhusūdana Sarasvatī's inclusion of Kāmaśāstra in Āyurveda seems to have the result of modern neglect of the study of the Śāstra. In modern times Kāmaśāstra meant only the śāstra of *union*, and of aphrodisiac mdicines. But in ancient times it meant much more. It included five hundred and eighteen fine arts, in fact all that contributed to make human life tolerable and pleasant. It included also domestic and social regulations of the best kind.

The ancient Kāmāsāstra was one of the four recognized divisions of the śāstras and ranked with Dharmaśāstra, Arthaśāstra and Mokṣśastra. The author of the Pañcatantra in ancient times would not venture to make it as Madhusūdana Sarasvatī did, a branch of Āyurveda which is but an Upaveda to the Artharva-Veda which goes under the head of Dharmaśāstra.

Subandhu.

Subandhu, I believe, belonged to Magadha under the Gupta emperors. All the speculations about his date by Fitzedward Hall and Mr. Grey of the Columbian University seem to be of not much avail. In the new series of the Journal and Proceedings of the Asiatic Society of Bengal Vol. I, I wrote in page 253—

In discoursing on the excellences of style Vāmana who belongs to the 9th century A.D. in his Kāvyālaṃkārasūtravṛtti quotes a verse as an example of the excellence named significance (sābhiprāyatva).

The verse or rather hemistich runs thus :—

Soyam samprati Candraguptatanayas Candraprakāśoyubā.

Jāto bhūpatirāśrayaḥ kṛtadhiyām diṣṭyā kṛtārthaśramah.

The son of Candragupta, the young rājā Candraprakāśa has now become the refuge of learned men and fortunately his endeavours are successful.

Commenting on this, the author says that the words "the refuge of learned men" are significant because they bring to mind the fact that Subandhu was one of his ministers Now there were two Candraguptas in the Gupta Line. Both were called Vikramāditya. The first was the founder of the empire and the second his grandson. The second Candragupta was a patron of learned men. Is it not likely that Subandhu served under one of his sons, Candraprakāśa ?

A controversy was raised in the Indian Antiquary in later years in which an attempt was made to make the words "ca Subandhu into Vasubandhu. But Mr. Narasiṃha Cāriar after consulting many manuscripts pointed out that it was *ca Subandhu* and not Vasubandhu. So my theory stands that Subandhu belonged to the reign of Candragupta II and the subsequent reigns. The only argument that can be urged against this theory is that Subandhu in one place writes *Nyāyasthitiriva Uddyotakarasarvasvā*[1] and so Subandhu knew Uddyotakara, the author of Nyāyavārttika, who, Vācaspati Miśra says, defended Vātsyāyana against the attacks of Diṇnāga[2]. But the facts so far known make the dates of Diṇnaga and

---

[17] Bell. Inded. p. 235. [18] Nyāyavārttika.

Uddyotakara later than that of Candragupta II. But I think these questions should be left open. One cannot get over the fact that Subandhu served under Candraprakāśa who was the son of Candragupta II and Subandhu in his preface to his Vāsavadattā laments that after the death of Virkramāditya[1] (Candragupta II) the world is going to rack and ruin. He is very bitter against *khalas* or envious people[2], who, I believe, brought about the ruin of his patron Candraprakāśa and of himself.

The plot interest of his work is nil and the author seems not to care much for it. All he cared for were his puns and in that he has shown a mastery never surpassed. He was conscious of his superiority and as prefaces are always written after the works themselves to which they are prefixed, he gives a criticism on his own work which is endorsed by all subsequent critics—

Sarasvatīdattavaraprasādaḥ cakre Subandhuḥ sujanaikabandhuḥ :

Pratyakṣaraśleṣamayaprabandhavinyāsavaidagdhyanidhirnibandham[3].

There is a pun in every letter as he says. The story is easily told.

Kandarpaketu, the son of Cintāmaṇi, a king, dreams in the morning of a damsel of exquisite beauty and goes in quest of her. He sleeps under the spreading arms of a mighty tree in the Vindhyas and awakening at midnight hears the quarrel of a parrot and his consort. She was angry for his coming late and he falters forth an apology—"I had been to Pāṭaliputra. There Vāsavadattā, the daughter of the king had a Svayambara but she rejected all the assembled princes and in a dream saw a youth of

---

[1] Preface Vase 10. [2] Ibid verses 7 & 8.

[3] Ibid 13.

great beauty and sent her female friend in quest of him. I have brought the female friend here. Kandarpaketu was greatly interested, he rose up and saw the young woman. She took him to Vāsavadattā where they learnt that the king had resolved to give her in marriage to another the next day. They fly away and hide themselves in a bower of creepers in the Vindhyas. But when the prince awakes in the morning he finds Vāsavadattā missing. He roams over great many places and at last finds a stone statue exactly of the same shape as the object of his love. He touches the statue and lo! she is Vāsavadattā. She tells him of her adventures. Anxious that the prince may have some food on awakening she goes into the wood to find roots and fruits and she was assailed by an army of wild tribes; luckily there was another army of wild tribes close by, and the two tribes fought with each other to obtain the possession of her person. But both armies perished, but at this time in came a Ṛṣi whose hermitage the armies in their fight had destroyed. Thinking that she was the cause of the destruction, he cursed her to be turned into stone. She implored him not to be angry as she was innocent and he said the curse will terminate at the touch of the prince she loves. There the story ends and they return to the capital of the prince's father where they passed their days happy and prosperous.

Āryabhaṭa.

Paṭaliputra was the birth-place of another very great man, namely, Āryabhaṭa, the father of scientific astronomy and mathematics of the Hindus. He was born in 476 A D. and wrote his Kālakriyāpāda here at the age of 23 that is, 499 A.D[1] He was a student of Greek Astronomy and the unique notation which goes in his name and which he gives in his Dasāgītikā seems to be an adaptation of the Greek system The consonants from ka to ma are valued at 1 to 25 and the eight vowels i, u, ṛ, e, l, ai, o, ou represent multiples of 100 each. Thus ka is 1, ki is 100, ku is 10,000, kṛ is 10,00,000, kl is 10,00,00,000, ke is 10,00,00,00,000, kai is 10,00,00,00,00,000. This is a modified form of the Greek System.

One of Āryabhata's works is called *Dasagītikā* from the fact that it consists of ten verses in the Gītikā metre which is a modification of the Āryā. His other work, the Aryasiddhāntika, consists of 108 verses and is divided in three sections Kālakriyāpāda, Golapāda and Gaṇitapāda In these two works the extent of which does not jointly go beyond 118 verses, Āryabhaṭa has explained the whole system of Hindu Astronomy. He is even more concise than the philosophical sūtras and is in strange contrast with the astronomical Siddhāntas which seem to have been written in prose and are very diffuse.

There seem to have been a conflict of Eras at the time when Āryabhata flourished. There was the Mālava Era in Western Malwa, the Gupta Era known in the Gupta Empire, the Saka Era, the Kalacuri Era and so on—all local and tribal eras. Not knowing in which to date his works which was meant for universal use among the Hindus he took up the Kaliyuga Era known to all. But in subsequent ages the Sāka Era was adopted by all astronomers in India. The reason is not far to seek for in India astronomy and astrology were, if not exclusively, very generally studied and professed by the Sākadvīpī Brahmins or Scythian priesthood—the old Magii—settled

---

[1] Kālakrīyapāda verse 10.

in India from remote ages, for neither the Brahmins or the Buddhists favoured astrologers. Buddha has expressly excluded Āstrology from Samyak Ājīva or proper livelihood.

Āryabhaṭa is said to have discovered the diurnal motion of the earth[1] which he thought to be spherical. I leave the explanation of these scientific matters to those who are making scientific investigations of Hindu Astronomy. But one thing is certain that it was about this time that the old Kṛttikā series of asterisms was discarded and the new series commencing from the 1st point of Aśvinī was adopted. The first point of Aśvinī recedes one degree or by one day in 73 years and it has receded twenty days now giving a total of twenty into seventy-three (20 × 73) that is, 1460 years. The point was on the equinoctial circle on the first day of Vaiśākha and now it is on the 10th of Chaitra. So the point was seen there 1460 years ago, that is, 1921-1460 that is 461 A.D. This is only an approximate calculation. If accurate calculation is made it will fall within the active period of Āryabhata's life.

Āryabhaṭa had many students and his next successor Lalla was one of his pupils and some say Varāhamihira, too, was his pupil.[2]

Aryabhaṭa had another celebrated astronomer as his contemporary. This was Varāhamihira. In his Vṛhajjātaka in the 26th chapter, he says that he was son of Ādityadāsa, that he was an Āvantaka, that he received his knowledge from his father and that he obtained a book from the Sun-God at Kāmpillaka or Kapitthaka. Bhaṭṭotpala tells us that he was a Māgadha *dvija*. Some say that he was a Magadvija, *i.e.*, one of the Magii long

---

[1] Pañca-Siddhāntikā preface, page, LVII.

[2] Gaṇakatarangiṇī Lalla and Varāha.

settled in India. From all this the late Paṇḍit Sudhākara Dvivedī in his Gaṇakataraṅginī infers (p. 12) that it is not impossible that Varāha was a Māgadha Brāhmin. He might have gone to Ujjain for livelihood. He studied with his father at his own house in Magadha and also studied the works of Aryabhaṭa there, he travelled to make himself known, he worshipped Sun-God at Kāmpillaka (Kalpi) and obtained a book from him. I acquired a man uscript of his son's work Pṛthuyasaḥ-Śāstra at Sāṁkhu the northernmost part of the Nepal valley, the opening verse of which says that the son Varāhamihira asked his father some questions while he was residing at the beautiful city of Kānyakubja on the Ganges.

Varāha might have retired to Kānyakubja in his old age to be on the Ganges and there imparted his knowledge to his son Pṛthuyasāḥ.

Āmarāja, the commentator of Khaṇḍanakhaṇḍakhādya says that Varāhamihira died in the Saka year 509 that is 587 A.D. Some people think that Varāha wrote his Panca-Siddhāntikā in 505 A.D. that is Saka 427. But this is impossible if we are to believe Amarāja. Varāha would then be only 18. Therefore Dr. Thibaut after carefully considering all the facts of the case thinks that 427 Śaka was the date when Lalla revised the Romaka-Siddhānta and that the Panca-Siddhānta was composed about 550 A.D. So Varāhamihira was a later contemporary and perhaps a student of Āryabhaṭa.

The Gaṇakataraṅginī has given a list of Varāha s works and thinks that the Vṛhat-Saṃhitā is his last work. It is an Encyclopœdic work. It treats not only of Astronomy and Astrology but of such subjects as gardening, agriculture, sculpture, strīlakṣaṇa, puruṣalakṣaṇa and so on. His great work is the Pañca-Sidhānta in which he gives a summary of all the Sidhāntas current in his time. They are five in number Paulisa, Romaka. Vāsiṣṭha, Paitāmaha and Sūryyasiddhānta. Varāha says that of these five Paulisa and Romaka have been explained by Lāṭadeva. The Siddhānta made by Paulisa is accurate. Near to it stands the Siddhānta proclaimed by Romaka, more accurate is the Sāvitra (Saura) and the two remaining are far from the truth.[1]

Kern says that the third Skandha of Jyotisa [2]namely, its Jātaka section has been borrowed from the Yavanas or Greeks. This is a fact. The Yavana-Jātaka of Yavanācāryya is still regarded as an authoritative work on the subject and there are other works like Mīnarāja Jātaka also taken from the Yavanas. I found in Nepal a manuscript of a Yavana-Jātaka written in the character of the tenth century on palm-leaf which contains the following statement at the end.—

Iti svabhāṣāracanābhiguptām
Viṣṇugraha.......................
......ratnākara-vāk-samudrāt
sudhāprāsa . . nvitatattvadṛṣṭiḥ.
Idam vabhāse niravadyavaktro
Horārkṣaśāstrm Yavaneśvaraḥ prāk
Sphujidhvajo nāma babhūva rājā
Ya Indravajrābhiridam cakāra.
Nārāyanāṅkendu mayādi dṛṣṭvā
Kṛtva caturbhir-matimān sahasraiḥ.
Yavana-Jātaka de.........parisamāptaḥ (Upendra-Vajrā Vṛttam).[2]

From this it is apparent that Yavaneśvara translated in Sanskrit a work which long remained hidden in his own language and that a **Rājā** named Sphujidhvaja

---

[1] Pañsa Chap. I. 3-4.

[2] See my paper in Ja & B part I, 1897.

rendered the Sanskrit prose into 4000 verses in Indravajrā metre. The translation was done in the 91st year of an unknown era and versifications in 191st year of the same era. Here is one independent evidence of the translation of Greek works in Sanskrit. Varāhamihira wrote a work on Jātaka or Horoscopy called Vṛhajjātaka. According to Gaṇakataraṅginī, in that work Varāha quotes from three works of the Greeks, Maya, Yavana and Manittha (Menetho) and he used many Greek words. All this shows the influence of Greek Astronomy on Indian Jyotiṣa. There is a saying in Gārgya that—

Mlechhā hi Yavanāsteṣu samyak śāstram-idam sthitam
Ṛṣivattepi pūjyante kim punar Vedaviddvijah.[3]

The next important book that was written in Magadha and at Pāṭaliputra was the Deśavalivivritiḥ in the 17th century. But from Varāhamihira in the 6th to the Deśavali in the 17th century is a great jump. But Magadha was not idle all these thousand years, rather its activity was intense. But unfortunately I cannot include that period of intense activity within the limited scope of my course of six lectures. So I have confined myself to strictly Brahmanical literature. The activity of the greater portion of these intervening 1000 years was confined to Buddhist literature. The rise of Nālanda in the 6th century is a great event in Indian history. Nālanda continued to command the attention of the world for more than five centuries when Vikramaśīla rose under the Pālas of Bengal and after Vikramaśīla we come to Jagaddala in Bengal. Nālanda used to send its learned monks all over the world and it drew students from all parts of the world specially the east. Yuan Chwang received his education here and on his return became the

[3] Gaṇait page 12.

second founder of Buddhism in China and his students carried the learning and religion of India to Japan, Korea, Mongolia and Siberia. When the Chinese ceased to come, came the Tibetans and Nalanda was the place where they began the translation of Sanskrit works in Tibetan which have preserved ten thousand of works from destruction and oblivion. Then the centre of Tibetan translation shifted to Vikramaśīla and thence to Jagaddala. The literature of Nalanda was in the beginning Mahāyānist and philosophical. It began Tantra which flourished in all its luxuriance at Vikramaśīla, the philosophy of which was more scholastic than that of Nalanda. In spite of Vikramaśīla and in spite of Jagaddala, Nalanda continued to flourish and we have manuscripts written there even in the eleventh century. I have got manuscripts copied at Baḍgāon in Bengali character which professor Bendall thought belonged to the 14th century, but which I think was copied before the Muhammadan conquest. Baḍgāon is well known to be an integral part of Nalanda. The Buddhist literature of this period is most interesting and most edifying but unfortunately it does not exist either in Sanskrit or in any Indian language. Most of the works exist only in the Tibetan and Chinese translations, some of them in original Sanskrit or Bengali have been found in Nepal and the western and even Southern India are contributing their quota of these Sanskrit works. Japan is doing much in contributing to the history of the literature of this period from Chinese translations and Tibet also is showing activity in that direction. A small body of very learned men with centres in London, Paris and Berlin are actively engaged in reconstructing a history of this period and I hope India specially this province which is most interested in it will not be lagging behind.

The last work which I wish to describe is the Deśāvali-vivrti, a gazetteer of Eastern India composed in the 17th century at Mogultuly in Patna under the patronage of a Chauhan Zamindar named Vijjala Bhūpati by his Paṇḍit, Paṇḍit Jagamohan. One may think that the compilation of the work was inspired by the Aini Akbari, but I think that the inspiration came from a different quarter and the inspiration is absolutely indigenous. Mithila's great poet Vidyāpati was a greatman, he was the first to write a gazetteer under the name of Bhūparikramā. He was followed by a Zamindar named Vikrama and his work is called Vikramaságara Vijjala Bhūpati appears to have been one of the descendents of Vikrama. So Vijjala's inspirations need not have come from Delhi. But unfortunately good manuscripts of the Gazetteer Literature are not yet forthcoming. Horace Hymen Wilson collected a mass of fragments and it is now deposited in the Sanskrit College Library, Calcutta and I acquired some fragments from Bankura which are now deposited in the Asiatic Society of Bengal. A study of these fragments have given us a mass of information about the Hindus three hundred years ago in Bihar, Bengal and the adjoining districts, their temples, their places of pilgrimage, their administration, their trade, their manufactures, their fortifications, their manners, their customs, their foibles and their habits. Vijjala was followed in in this department of work by the Rājā of Pañcakot whose poet Rāmakavi wrote a work under the name of Pāṇḍavadigvijaya.

Here I bring my course of six lectures on the Magadha Literature to a close. When I undertook to deliver my lectures I thought I would have to fill up most of my pages with the history of Buddhist and Jaina literature of Magadha for I thought it would be difficult, nay impossible for me to locate any work of Hindu Literature except Kautilya's in Magadha. But luckily the Kāvya-Mīmāṃsā of Rājaśekhara and the Harṣacarita of Vāṇa helped me to locate a number of works there and these works instead of being of sectarian interest are such that all Indians, nay the whole world may be interested in them. I have, therefore, neglected the sects and selected such works only as are of general interest.

It would have afforded me the greatest pleasure if I could have finished these lectures during the administration of Sir Edward Gait who took a keen interest in everything Magadhan and always encouraged me in my researches in this province. But as it is he will read these pages in his retirement and have the satisfaction to know that his humble friend has not neglected to fulfil the task imposed on him.

HARAPRASAD SASTRI.